PREDRAG MATVEJEVIĆ

OUR
DAILY
BREAD

**A MEDITATION ON THE CULTURAL AND SYMBOLIC
SIGNIFICANCE OF BREAD THROUGOUT HISTORY**

Translated from the Croatian by
Christina Pribichevich-Zorić

istrosbooks

Venditore di Pane

TABLE OF CONTENTS

I.
BREAD AND
THE BODY

Bread was born in ashes, on stone. It is older than books, and older than writing. Its first names are carved on clay tablets, in bygone languages. Part of its past is buried under ruins, along with its history, divided among countries and peoples. For the story of bread is rooted in the past and in history; it is connected to both, while identifying with neither.

Perhaps it was a brick that provided the first bread-maker with a model for the loaf. Earth and dough once sat side by side on the fire, on the far side of our collective memory.

No one knows when or where the first ear of grain sprouted, but its appearance must have attracted attention and aroused curiosity. The ordered distribution of the grains on the stem served as an example of harmony, measure, perhaps even equality, while the variety and quality of the various cereals revealed their differences, their virtues and probably also a hierarchy.

Traces of the first cereals can be found on several continents. In ancient times, they thrived in the plains of the "Fertile Crescent", a region that spanned modern-day Iraq, Syria, Lebanon, Israel, Palestine, Jordan, the north-east and Nile Valley regions of Egypt, together with the south-eastern region of Turkey and the western fringes of Iran. Over the Euphrates shone a star called Anunit; over the Tigris it was the "Swallow star". Their brilliance, it was believed, contributed to the fertility of Mesopotamia. Wheat grew in the Horn of Africa, between the Great Sea and the Sea of Reeds, near Aksum, Asmara, Addis Ababa. The desert ends in the plateaus of Ethiopia and Eritrea, where the climate is milder, the earth more fertile. Nearby is the source of the Blue Nile, which flows down to meet the other tributary of this wondrous river, the White Nile. The region enjoys an abundance of sunshine. "Bread is the fruit of the earth blessed by light," says the German poet, Friedrich Hölderlin.

Perhaps it was to Egypt that cereals first came from the Middle East, but they followed other routes, as well. Carbonized seeds have been discovered in the western parts of the African desert, in fire pits more than 8,000 years old; here, too, somebody had once sown and reaped. Desert tribes from the Sahara, which once resembled the savannah, approached the Nile by trying to follow the riverbank. They found it criss-crossed with streams where nomads could quench their thirst and camels and gazelles could drink water. And so the Bedouins stopped in the oases, before continuing on their way. These journeys and stories, too, are older than history.

The origins of bread go back to the times when nomads became settlers, hunters became shepherds and both farmed. Some moved from hunting-ground to hunting-ground and from pasture to pasture; others cleared and worked the land: the vocation of Cain versus that of Abel. The nomadic life veered towards adventure, while the life of the settler required patience. Those wall drawings discovered in caves that were once used by nomads often depict long or broken lines that come from somewhere and lead somewhere else; moving from the unknown to the unknown. The drawings done by farmers, on the other hand, tend to be rounder, the spaces more delineated, with a discernible centre.

The sowing and reaping divided time into periods, the year into months, then into weeks and days. Routes shortened distances between places. Huts were built in the valleys, while denser dwelling areas were constructed by rivers. The digging of furrows changed the appearance of the fields, and allowed ears of grain to cover the land. The landscape changed from one generation to the next.

∞∞∞

The *Epic of Gilgamesh*, written in cuneiform script around 1800 BCE, mentions the bread eaten by the protagonist Enkidu, a skilled hunter who was accustomed to eat game. This mountain man who ate grass with the gazelles and sucked the milk of wild beasts, was surprised when he tasted bread for the first time. The journey from raw to cooked grain was a long one, and the man who made bread was different from his ancestors: He found himself standing on the threshold of history.

From the beginning of cultivation, the farmer had to keep his eye on the ploughed land, waiting for a yield. He scanned the sky, fearing for his crop, and he understood that the earth and the sky raised questions but offered no answers. As a result, different explanations and different belief systems came into being and spread. "Bread belongs to mythology," said Hippocrates.

In the Garden of Eden, Eve picked the fateful apple and offered it to Adam, incurring God's punishment: "By the sweat of your face you shall eat bread." The division of labour was dictated by necessity. The man worked in the field, the woman worked in the garden. He sowed and reaped, while she kneaded and baked. "Women sprinkled much white flour upon it – a meal for the labourers," it says in the *Iliad*, while in the *Odyssey* the author underscores the difference between those who eat bread and those who eat lotuses – the *lotophagi* or "barbarians" who couldn't even speak properly. While some salted their meals and others refrained from it, both bread and salt were unknown to the Cyclops Polyphemus.

According to the Old Testament, Gideon's defeat of the Midianites was inspired by a dream one of his soldiers had about barley bread: "he made unleavened cakes of an *ephah* of flour" – one of which tumbled down into the enemy camp. Pausanias also left to posterity the legend of the man who helped win the Battle of Marathon, midway between Athens and Karystos: "A man of rustic appearance and dress" charged at the overpowering Persians, brandishing his ploughshare, doubled over like a reaper. No one knew who he was or where he came from, not even the oracle of Delphi. When consulted, it merely responded with this sibylline message: "Honour Echetlaeus (he of the Plough-tail)." Pausanias then goes on to tell us that "a monument of white marble" was erected in his honour.

Periander, the tyrant of Corinth, sent a messenger to Thrasybulus in Miletus, asking for advice on how best to rule. Thrasybulus did not reply, but while speaking to the messenger in a wheat field, cut off all the tallest ears of wheat and threw them away. Hearing an account of the episode, Periander understood, followed the advice and killed the most prominent citizens of Corinth. According to the Book of Genesis, the pharaoh also dreamt of bread: "In my dream there were three baskets of white bread on my head" and "seven ears of corn, rank and good", threatened by the thin and hollow ones. Joseph reminded the pharaoh that after abundance comes austerity, and he proposed building huge storehouses for the grain, to secure bread for the lean years.

And so we see the ear of grain and images of bread move from reality to dreams, and from dreams to reality, finding their place in the soul and in the body.

The prophet Isaiah foresaw a time when people "shall beat their swords into ploughshares, and their spears into pruning hooks". But as we know, the heavens did not heed the prophet's words. The earth turned a deaf ear and faith failed to disarm the warrior. The power structures gave more support to soldiers than to the sowers.

From time immemorial, parasites have been a threat to grain and flour, to bread and the human body that it nourishes. Their names have come to symbolize misfortune, trouble, devastation. Darnel, ryegrass and weeds are mentioned in the scriptures, as is mildew, a blight that is also referred to as rust or soot. Caterpillars and cockroaches plagued crops, rats and rodents infested granaries. We do not even know the names of some of these pests, but ants are not among them. Naturalists of the past, like Darwin, certainly paid them tribute. Everybody knows that an ant carries a load that is heavier than its own self, and those industrious insects have certainly taught us lessons, inspired comparisons and even metaphors: in order to survive, farmers were "as industrious as ants"; they gathered "like ants" in the field and on the threshing floor; and a good man wouldn't step on an ant. Perhaps it is these very insects themselves that gave an example to people of how to gather and store grains for the coming days.

"The universe begins with bread," Diogenes Laertius quotes Pythagoras as saying. Preserved remains of grains and bread have been discovered next to sarcophagi and urns in graves, in pyramids, in places where one bid farewell to this life in the hope of a celestial, eternal life. There are also numerous vestiges and legends to show that separating the wheat from the chaff and weeds, the grain from the chaff and hay, the flour from bran and particles, the pure from the impure, are all age-old actions.

Bread is the product of both nature and culture. It was the condition for peace and the cause of war, the promise of hope and the reason for despair. Religions blessed it. People swore by it. Countries without enough bread experience discontent, but then again countries with nothing but bread do not fare much better, which calls to mind the adage, "One cannot live on bread alone" – a phrase that has echoed down through the centuries.

Food security, however, has always been an issue associated with bread. Century after century famine raged in various parts of the world, disturbing the natural connection between the body and bread. The *Epic of Gilgamesh* mentions the "seven years of drought" in Uruk, when not a grain was to be found in the husk. Both the Talmud and the Bible comment on the "seven lean cattle" and "seven lean years". In the Old Testament, the First Book of Kings writes: "if there be in the land famine, if there be pestilence, blasting, mildew, locust, or if there be caterpillar … whatsoever plague, whatsoever sickness there be." At the turn of the Middle Ages, the Byzantine historian Procopius of Caesarea described crowds of people roaming around, emaciated and sallow-faced, so hungry that sometimes they ate each another.

Year 18 of the Hijri (640 CE) was proclaimed in Medina "the year of drought" – *am al-ramad*. During the reign of the Ikshidid, Islamicized Egypt also experienced periods of famine and misfortune, each worse than the last: in the years 341 and 343 of the Hijri (953 and 955 CE), and again in 352 and 360 of the same calendar (963 and 971 CE). Poor harvests were the consequence of many factors: the low water level of the Nile, conflicts between proprietors and slaves, corrupt scribes and clerks, the impoverishment of villagers and peasants, the revolt of the Bedouins and contagions that spread through cities and villages. An Arabic record noted that there were so many bodies they didn't even manage to bury them all. According to the writings of Ibn Said, inhabitants of the desert even mixed crushed bones with their bread flour. During the reign of Al Mustansir Billah (1029–94 CE), the famine lasted a full seven years.

The fateful number seven is often associated with similar disasters.

Famine continued to decimate the population under the rule of sultan Al Nasir Muhammad bin Qalawun, in the eighth century of the Hijri (thirteenth/fourteenth century CE). Historians have recorded that every bakery had four guards to protect the millers and bakers. They carried clubs and were ready to stop anyone from stealing grain and flour. Matters got even worse under the sultanate of Al-Mu'ayyad Shaykh (1412–21 CE), when almost half the population died of starvation. It was during this time that bread was given names of ill omen such as *hubz al-kurud* ("monkey bread"), *hubz al kalb* ("dog bread") and *hubz al dub* ("bear bread"). If you wanted to help or save the life of a friend or a guest, you would give them a "guarantee loaf" – *raghifu emani*.

Even today, in Egypt the Arabic and Coptic word *aysh* means both bread and life – the body that immortalizes life.

An integral part of our civilization, the knowledge of grain and bread was something to be passed down from generation to generation along with the tools and instruments people bequeathed to their progeny, that had a familiarity in appearance or in purpose. The "crib" for kneading dough looks like a baby's cradle, like the bed in which we sleep, like the coffin in which our bodies will lie, like the boat that will take us from one shore to the other. Sieves and sifters, colanders and strainer nets are all related. These tools and accessories evolved over long, uncertain periods of time: from tinder and fire to hearths and ovens; from blade stones to forged knives; from deer horns, perhaps first used to loosen virgin soil, to ploughshares and real ploughs; from mortar and pestle to millstones powered by water or wind, or by slaves and donkeys. These tools, each according to its nature and purpose, marked the passing of time and the history of bread. And with them came amphoras, sacks and baskets to carry and transport the grain and flour. And once it was prepared, the stone or brick oven produced dough in its final form – bread that could be served at the table, offered at feasts, blessed at the altar, begged for in the street or stolen on the highway.

And always it was accompanied by song, prayer, supplication.

The fate of bread was often different from the history that went with it, from the past that gave birth to it. Growth and development are not always in step, as evidenced by the traces they have left. They are often scattered and unclear. So it is often down to stories to try to gather the scattered traces and give them shape. Memories of bread are better preserved than bread itself, for the body of bread is also mortal.

For centuries, public bakeries would spring up in city squares and villages. Like threshing floors, they became places where people could meet and talk. News was passed on, events related – who had had a baby, whose parent had died, whose daughter or son was getting married. Before placing the dough into the oven, it was impressed with a special stone, wooden or metal stamp bearing the name, coat of arms or cross of the person to whom it belonged. Often the loaf of bread bore a cross on its body.

◌◌◌

Across the globe peoples have sown and harvested in different seasons of the year, in months that had more or less rain, in wind or in frost. In the Valley of the Nile, rye was sown in late autumn and harvested in the middle of spring, as its fast growth left room in the field for other crops. The star known by the Egyptians as Sothis – perhaps the same one we call Sirius – would herald the water level, be it high or low, and warn of floods and droughts. The wheat germinated in furrows after the autumn rains so that it could be harvested by the summer.

Maturation and yield were linked to the cycles of the Zodiac, the position of the sun and the moon, the stars and constellations. The "Shepherd's Star" (Capella in the constellation of Auriga) appeared late into dusk and vanished early into dawn. Wheat was sown under the sign of Virgo and harvested under the sign of Leo. Barley had a shorter cycle, beginning at almost the same time, during Virgo, and ending during Cancer. Rye, which grows even faster, was from Aries to Leo, a period of around 100 days. Various interpretations regarding seeds and the harvest, and sometimes conception and childbirth, are attributed to Virgo, when shooting stars are said to visit the heavens and archangels to descend to earth.

Along coastlines and in a good part of the hinterland, the belief persisted that the phases of the moon affect dough and the leaven it contains – just as they affect the tide, our body and our moods. The only thing more important than the signs of the Zodiac and position of the stars was perhaps the belief that these signs and positions were real and influential. In the Levant, time was measured and the years counted according to the lunar calendar, before the solar calendar was established.

Anaxagoras of Clazomenae was one of the first philosophers of ancient Greece to notice and describe the actual connection between bread and the human body: "Let us consider a loaf of bread. It is composed of vegetable matters and helps to nourish our body. However, the constituent parts of the human body are multiple: skin, flesh, blood, veins, sinews, cartilages, bones, hair ... How, then, could it happen that the uniformly constituted bread should produce this rich multiplicity of objects? A change of qualities is not possible, so that the sole remaining hypothesis is that the bread that nourishes us already contains the countless forms of matter which the human body displays." The Roman translator of this ancient text tried to elaborate on its meaning: this philosopher went from bread to grain, from grain to the earth, from both to water, fire, down to the first elements and principles. Hence, the body and food can be connected to temperament: sanguine and choleric, phlegmatic and melancholic.

Gregory of Nyssa in Cappadocia, an early Christian preacher, saw the relationship between the body and bread in a similar way to the materialist Anaxagoras: "If a person sees bread, he sees, in a certain sense, the human body, because the bread that enters the body becomes the body itself."

In this way, it has often been said that the body and bread understand one another, for bread engages all of our senses, each in its own way. The most often mentioned is the smell of bread, its delicious odour. Once it reaches the nose, it enters the body, where the trace it leaves mingles with memories of childhood, youth and home.

The taste of bread is also closely linked to memories, recent and old. Does it taste the way it used to? Is it better or worse than we remember? Why is or isn't it the way we remember it, the way it should be?

The touch of bread is not something one forgets, either. Is the crust smooth or crisp, is the middle soft or already stale? How do the hand, palm and fingers pick it up, hold it, break it? To whom do we offer and give it? How, when and where?

Sight has its own criteria. What does the bread before us look like and how could or should it look? Is it similar to bread we have already seen in real life or imagined in our dreams? Is it different? Throughout history, the eyes of the hungry have often shed tears for a crust of bread.

Perhaps the hardest sensory link to identify is the connection between hearing and bread. For bread is quiet, mute. It doesn't make any noise, but noise does come from the people gathered around it. When a slice of bread is dropped or falls off the table it makes hardly a sound, which may be an indication of something else. For, there are moments when bread can be heard. If a child dropped a piece of bread on the floor, her mother would tell her to pick it up and kiss it. When bakers or homemakers removed a loaf of bread from the oven they would often tap it with their finger to see if it was done. The resulting sound, hollow or not, or both, would give them the answer.

The way bread is placed on the table may be a vestige of an old, more or less forgotten ritual. How bread is handled, when following Jewish or Christian tradition, again reflects the relationship between bread and the body. In some Islamic countries, one presses one's thumb into the dough before placing it on the hearth or in the oven, to show that it was made by the human hand. In olden times, a piece from the soft middle of the bread was placed on cuts to staunch the bleeding and close the wound. In peacetime, when countries were not at war with each other or themselves, people would gather breadcrumbs into the palm of their hand and keep them. For the birds.

∽∽∽

The oldest names saved from oblivion by the oral and written word tell us how bread was made, the kind of flour that was used, as well as the kind of oven. Some names indicate the spiritual and earthly values vested in it: the "bread of life", "bread of tears" and the "living bread" of the scriptures; bread as "the Host", "blessed" and "sacrificial" bread, "bread of angels", the "bread of friendship" mentioned in the Psalms. Even for the dead, there is bread, the hard and unsweetened "bread for the dead" of All Souls Day. And not forgetting the "holy bread", ceremonious and austere, on All Saints Day. These are only part of the catalogue of epithets that has been passed down to us through Christian ritual.

Attitudes to the body and bread depended on one's world outlook, beliefs and faith. The Iranian prophet Zarathustra valued the soul but not the body. Not wishing to contaminate the earth, his followers placed corpses in "towers of silence", leaving them there for carrion birds to dispense with. The Neoplatonist Plotinus was embarrassed by his body, most probably because of some of its animalistic functions. For this very reason, when a Roman sculptor wanted to make a bust of him, Plotinus refused. Even Seneca tried to avoid the conflict between body and soul: "The wise man, as well as the seeker of wisdom, is no doubt dependent on his body, but he is absent with respect to that greater part of himself (i.e. his body) and he directs his thoughts to the higher things." St. Paul wrote: "God hath tempered the body together, having given more abundant honour to that part which lacked: That there should be no schism in the body; but that the members should have the same care one for the other." Yet in the Judaeo-Christian tradition, bread became the reconciler of body and soul, since the Eucharist elevated it to saintliness.

Like the human body, grains age. And in the end, they both decompose. The quality of the grain depends on the type of seed and fertility of the soil in which it grows. Black soil is considered to be the best. Some once popular and valued grains have almost disappeared or died out, grains such as *shumara* and the "white wheat of Yamamah". Possibly the last grains of "emmer wheat" were discovered within the walls of the pyramids in Dahshur. From their outward appearance it was thought they had been preserved but the seeds inside them were dead. Even the most fertile soil could not produce an ear of this wheat.

The Egyptians called the fertile land bordering the Nile *khemi*. The root of the word may come from the word chemistry, or perhaps it was eclipsed by another similar term. The people who made bread for thousands of years knew little about the chemical processes and changes that occur when producing it: the relationship between proteins and carbohydrates; the conversion of carbohydrates into sugar, and sugar into alcohol; the alcohol, which in concert with leaven or yeast, produces gasses that raise the dough and make it porous; the way that the middle of the bread becomes lighter and softer, while the crust becomes crunchy or hard. All this is what gives the bread its shape, its taste and its smell. Its body and soul.

The best bread-makers were careful about the quality of the water they used, whether it was from a river or well, from a spring, a stream or a lake. Whether it streamed down from the mountain or flowed through a valley. How fresh or stagnant, cold or tepid, clear or cloudy it was. Whether the sediment had been removed from the water or retained. Only seawater is not used when making bread, because its very composition is different. Even sea salt, or any coarse salt, does not dissolve easily. When mixed with dough, it turns grey or sometimes even blue. In some countries they dissolve it by "washing" or "soaking" it in fresh water, or by placing it on the fire, where it sputters or dissipates. The best solution is to grind it before using it in the dough crib. In ancient Alexandria, they had mills to grind large clumps of sea salt, where it would become as fine as flour and gave the bread a special taste. In regions where the sea retreated long ago, the salt sometimes retains the fragrance of lavender, rosemary, sage or immortelle, imbuing the dough with it, and thus the bread. This "fleur de sel" is considered to have curative properties for the body.

It has to be said that there is also no small amount of salt in the sweat of ploughmen, sowers and bakers. And in human tears.

Yeast, composed of living cells that are invisible to the naked eye, is absorbed well by the body. Beer yeast is one of the oldest in existence. It was used in ancient times by the Babylonians and Egyptians. The Hebrews discovered it during their time in enslavement under the pharaohs. According to ancient lore, bread yeast may have come into being by accident, when somebody poured a cup of beer into a crib of dough. Some attribute the event to a distracted woman, others to a drunken man, but we shall never know the true story. What we do know is that yeast, with the addition of air and oxygen, becomes the starter, a pre-ferment used in indirect methods of bread-making – also called "mother dough". Although its components are few, it produces energy that can raise a weight much greater than its own. Bread, beer and wine have different kinds of yeast – similar to one another, yet all different. Even the smallest piece of yeast retains its properties and can transmit them to another piece. It simultaneously renews and consumes itself until it finally depletes itself.

The quality of the bread also depends on the kind of wood used to heat the oven or hearth. Usually these were branches collected from the local area, not far from the fields. Oak and beech, ash, poplar and elm trees grow more in the hinterland than by the sea. Hornbeam, holly-oak, spruce and shrub can be found everywhere, except in the desert. Pinewood was seldom used in bakeries, most likely because of the amount of resin it contains. Cypress trees are spared, perhaps out of respect for the places in which they usually grow – cemeteries and places of worship. The wood of fir trees burns quickly, producing flames rather than heat. In ancient times, Lebanese cedars were used to build ships, but their bark and shavings – left over from making the beams and boards of the keel and deck – were also used to heat the oven. Wild olive trees burn well and have a nice smell, especially when their branches are left to dry in the sun and wind. Once the embers burnt red, the experienced baker would toss a handful of fragrant grasses on them. In the desert, where trees are few if any, the Bedouins would bake flatbread on slabs of stone or hardened sand, and for fuel also use camel dung. These methods date back to biblical times, and the body has become accustomed to it.

Sometimes the bread cracks open in the oven, but if it is made properly it retains its taste. The Roman emperor Marcus Aurelius noted in his meditation "To Himself", written before death caught up with him in the ancient Roman military camp of Vindobona (modern-day Vienna): "We should remark the grace and fascination that there is even in the incidentals of Nature's processes. When a loaf of bread, for instance, is in the oven, cracks appear in it here and there; and these flaws, though not intended in the baking, have a rightness of their own, and sharpen the appetite (*cupiditas edendi*)." These "cracks" create "hips" on the body of the bread, and it has to be said that gourmets love them.

And let us not forget the heel or end-piece of a loaf. It is not sliced off with a knife, it is broken off with one's hands. It is tasted with curiosity and eaten with delight. Even when stale, it retains its taste, if only as a memory. Children especially love the heel, because the heel is more than just a piece of the bread.

The colour of bread can differ, as well. Sometimes its crust is brown, at others quite dark, whereas the middle of the loaf is lighter. Despite their names, white bread isn't completely white nor is black bread completely black. The ruling dynasties of ancient Egypt included dark-skinned pharaohs from Nubia and Eritrea. The colour of their skin did not influence their choice of bread, nor the grains used to make it.

The relationship between the body and bread can also be seen reflected in certain customs, rituals and laws. In the Middle East and its environs, in Hellenic cities and islands, especially Crete and Cyprus, in the Maghreb and the Mashreq, women were sometimes forbidden from kneading dough if they were menstruating. Men, meanwhile, were required to shave their arms up to their elbows, cover themselves, and wear a cap to prevent any strand of hair or bead of sweat from falling onto the dough. Only "clean" bodies were permitted to approach the dough crib or bread oven.

Over the centuries, awareness of the beneficial effects of hygiene on one's health and beauty spread from East to West, and back from West to East. And, here, bread played a special role. The movements and gestures involved in making bread were repeated and adapted from one era to the next. Men did the hard work in bakeries. Women used their finer skills at home. Descriptions and visual depictions show the body bending over cribs in which flour and water are mixed with salt and yeast. The weight shifts from the back and shoulders onto the arms and elbows, from the arms and elbows onto the hands and palms, from the hands and palms onto the dough. The body's work and effort is invested in the bread itself and the end of the process was often followed by moments of joy, albeit sometimes short-lived.

Sowers and reapers, too, bend their bodies when they work, staring ahead at what still remains to be done, and looking back at how much of the field they have covered, making sure that the seeds have fallen into the furrow, that the spacing is right. Some of these movements have already disappeared from everyday contemporary life, and it must be said that the body may be all the poorer for it.

However, in bread-making our busiest body part is always the hands. They sow, reap, separate the wheat from the chaff with a coarse sieve, separate the flour from the bran with a fine sieve, knead the dough, place it in the oven and remove it when it has been baked. In Emmaus, a town mentioned in the Gospel of Luke as the place where Jesus appeared after his death and resurrection, the disciples recognized the resurrected Christ by the way he picked up, held and broke the offered loaf of bread.

Geometry followed the evolution of bread in the shapes into which it could be formed: round, rectangular, triangular, square, oval or pyramidal. Depending on the occasion, the imagination worked to shape bread like a boat, a fish, an egg, a half-moon, a doll, braids or plats, even into the shape of a little house, or the body of a man or woman, or just the male or female genitals. Figurines made of bread dough, painted in naïve colours, can be found in crèches, churches, at fairs and in souks. Prisoners often modelled chess pieces out of breadcrumbs and those who liked games of chance, especially cards, used them to make the heads of "queens", "jacks" or the fatal "queen of spades".

The profiles of dancers are visible on the oldest drawings and sculptures, urns and reliefs, and bread, too, has always played a certain role in entertainment involving the body and spirit. This connection between bread and dance has long been known. In the biblical story of the exodus of the Jews from Egypt, after Miriam crossed the Red Sea, she picked up the tambourine and all the women followed her with music and dance. In ancient Egypt, the dancers' bellies were always bare, mimicking those of the women who kneaded the dough for bread. The Phoenicians were known to love dancing – being both able sailors and talented bakers, they brought their passions to the shores they reached. Before performing at important ceremonies, which could be physically exhausting, dancers were advised to eat as much bread as they could so as to keep their bodies supple. Before competing, Roman athletes ate a special bread called *panis athletarum*, which was usually rye or barley bread without yeast, in order to keep their muscles hard and strong.

Bread and the body came together in dance and competition.

A good diet is always a combination of knowledge and care. The moderation it requires is not the same as fasting, and our efforts to follow a diet are useful if not always successful. Hippocrates maintained that good barley bread – *maza* – fortifies the body, is good for the digestion and prevents diarrhoea. He recommended it especially in the hot months of summer. The father of medicine advised his contemporaries: "Fermented bread is lighter in digestion and passes easily through the body ... The largest loafs are most nutritious because they are less dried out by the fire ... Oven bread is more nutritious than griddle bread and spit-bread because it is less burnt by the fire." The Hippocratic diet also mentions the kinds of bread that are best for preserving one's health and avoiding illness: *synkomostos*, made of wholemeal, unsifted flour, helps the intestines work better; *aleton katharon*, made of fine sieved flour, is nourishing but harder to digest; *xylos*, which contains yeast juice, is healthy and is not heavy on the stomach; *ipnitai* are rolls baked in an open oven, but one must be careful not to overbake them because then they become hard; *klibanitai* stick to the sides of the vessel, have a soft crust and are recommended for older people; *enkryfiai*, baked in ashes, and dry and tasty, retain the nutritious qualities of the grain; *semidalis* contains semolina and is good for the digestion; *hondros*, made with wheat flour and tasty, is harder to digest. Bread even had medicinal purposes, and different kinds of bread were recommended to the sick to bring down a fever, make urinating easier or regulate one's bowel movements.

The many recommendations made by Hippocrates and his followers show the degree to which ancient medicine, of which diet was an integral part, took into account the relationship between the body and bread.

Acron of Agrigento, the ancient Sicilian healer, established his own teachings on dietary nutrition but failed to attract a sufficient number of followers to the island. The Schola Medica Salernitana was a medieval medical school, the first and most important of its kind; it was founded in the ninth century and rose to prominence in the tenth century, becoming the most important source of medical knowledge in Western Europe at the time. Here they resorted to verse in their instructions about bread, advising everyone to take care of their body and "follow a diet": *Omnibus assuetam jubeo servare diaetam*. It recommends: "Eat not your bread too stale, nor eat it hot/ a little leaven, hollow baked and light."

The famous twelfth-century school of medicine in Montpellier offered similar advice, but in prose.

∞∞

Historians say that during the fourteenth century Europe lost one-third of its population in seven years. The roads were strewn with unburied corpses. In the worst times of famine and despair, people used their ingenuity to grind anything they thought could replace grain, flour and bread. In their endeavour to keep making bread, they did not just resort to the poorest varieties of grain, such as spelt, oats, millet and buckwheat; records show that people also used huge amounts of poppyseed, acorns, carobs and chestnuts, chickpeas, broad beans and lentils, sesame, sunflower, caraway, coriander and anise seeds and who knows what else. Such mixtures produced a sluggishness and drowsiness in both the body and mind very different from the usual nutritional value of ordinary bread. More upsetting still, certain weeds and roots, grasses and nettles, mixed with wild legumes and vetch, and sometimes even with sand, earth and sawdust, had a fatal effect. Crushed or ground and then turned into a mash that was either boiled or baked, they caused fevers, nightmares, dizziness, insomnia, visions of witches, vampires, "black angels" and all sorts of delusions. There were epidemic waves of scrofula, convulsions, coughing, diarrhoea, delirium, the black plague, and the swollen, red lymph node (buboes) in the armpit of a person with bubonic plague. Flies, lice, bedbugs and various vermin carried infections from one region to another. A terrible time for all people, from the numberless vagrants and beggars roaming from village to village and fair to fair in the hope of stealing or cajoling out of someone a crust of bread, to those behind prison bars – inmates who lived on bread and water, losing weight and becoming weak, yet managing to survive, sometimes for a long time, because even the poorest bread provided what their bodies needed. When the pilgrims travelling to the Holy Land strayed from their path and saw the pyramids, they were said to have imagined that they were seeing huge granaries and to have envied the locals for what they thought was their glut of bread.

The world of medicine has always tried to help the starving and sick. Hippocrates had already described how hunger and illness could affect the body and its movements; the same hands that kneaded the dough and baked the bread would make the same movements even when there was nothing there to knead or bake. Medieval physicians and pharmacists provided advice and instructions, advising against hunger, *Pracepta contra famem*, but it was all in vain when famine ruled. There was even a sixteenth-century Italian comedy titled *Banchetto de' malcibati* ("Banquet of the Poorly Fed"). Performed as part of the *Commedia dell'arte*'s repertoire in city after city, the play's jester, *giullare*, endowed the characters with such ironic names as Lady Famine, Messer Small Harvest, Lady Poverty and so on. The wobbly table in performances of the "The Court of Miracles" held only scraps of bread. The medieval myth of "The Land of Cockaigne", promising a fantastic land of plenty, mutated into a pathetic carnival. Processions became funerals; monasteries, alms houses; prayers, laments; pilgrims, martyrs; and ascetics, corpses. Poverty identified with popular theatre on the open stage and the pundits heralded the end of the world, while the chroniclers foresaw the Apocalypse.

Poverty and destitution were also at the root of the picaresque novel, a genre of prose fiction that depicts the adventures of a hero of low social class who lives by his wits in a corrupt society, which was popular from the mid-1500s until the eighteenth century. The *picaro* (Spanish: *picaresca*, from *pícaro*, "rogue" or "rascal") leaves his native town with his face and eyes hollowed out by hunger, for it has been a long time since he tasted even a crumb of bread. He leaves with no destination, roaming around markets, fairs and alms houses, living by his wits by "pinching" whatever he can find. "Bread and bulls" (*pan y toros*) is the Spanish version of an old Latin saying (*panem et circenses* – "bread and circuses"). The character of the student who has not yet graduated is preserved in the annals of history, he who knows the works of Aristotle and Avicenna but not anything that will be of practical help to him. He is called a *capiggorista* because of the cloak around his shoulders and cap on his head. Thin and frail, he is always rushing somewhere, looking for something, usually a crust of bread. The records show that Madrid's markets, and especially its bakeries, were repeatedly ravaged, and in Castilla, vagabonds were called "lost bread" (*pan perdido*) and beggars, "grasshoppers" (*saltamontes*). Begging, like prostitution, required a permit that was strictly limited to the given area.

Cervantes' "Knight of the Sad Countenance" sought consolation in bread: "All sorrows are less with bread" (*los duelos con pan son menos*). Perhaps that Knight of the Sad Countenance fought windmills because they hadn't ground enough grain to feed the starving. And perhaps Sancho Panza rode his donkey dreaming of bread.

Like writers, painters depicted bodies that were weak and pale, looks that were sad and lost. In his youth, El Greco travelled from the island of Crete, where he was born in 1541, to Toledo, where he was to become famous. He painted the starving Christians he encountered along the way. In Florence, pre-Renaissance paintings bore witness to the suffering of the city's people. Venetian artists were more cheerful. *La Serenissima*, which imported and sold grains, managed to avoid the disaster of famine, if not of the plague. It is easily noted that virtually all the bodies depicted on Byzantine icons from the late Middle Ages are emaciated.

The Jews expelled from Spain by the Inquisition were accused, among other things, of wanting to bring Christians closer to their own faith by offering them unleavened bread with the coming of Passover. The non-Christians being transported by Genovese galley ships to the Ottoman Empire or the countries of the Maghreb, the Balkans, Istanbul, Smyrna, Thessaloniki or Sarajevo, cried out for a piece of ship's biscuit even if roaches had already nibbled at it first. However, the Sephardim and Marranos (from the word *marrano*, which means "pig" in Spanish) did not forget their *matzah* or how their ancestors had made it. Some moved northwards, where the great Rembrandt saw their wan, gaunt faces. Indeed, some of his drawings followed the work of the scholar

Rabbi Menasseh ben Israel, with whom he shared the bread of friendship. In Amsterdam at that time, one could also hear the voice of Baruch Spinoza: *Deus sive natura*, "God or nature". Bread is connected to both.

Even the new age did not manage to escape old scourges. One year there was too much rain, the next there was drought – and the third saw frost. In one place the seeds died, in another the ears of grain rotted and the result was that the granaries stood empty. Records show that there were more lean years to come. The summers of 1420, 1693, 1816 and 1819 are marked in black. In 1709, the winter lasted until the middle of spring, destroying all the grains and claiming hundreds of thousands of lives. It seemed to many like a second "ice age", although shorter this time, but just as deadly, encompassing not only the northern regions of Europe, but also the south, and even islands like Sardinia and Majorca, and parts of Sicily and Cyprus suffered unprecedented weather conditions.

In desperation, seafarers set their sights on India, in the hope of finding rice fields there. Instead they landed in the Americas, and found corn, which is easy to cultivate, quick to grow and is abundant in grain. They brought it back, along with potatoes, which helped to alleviate hunger in the old continent. And so corn became the main ingredient of daily bread as food for the body.

〇〇〇

Over time, modern machines increasingly started doing the work of sowers and reapers, millers and bakers, women and mothers. Production became "industrialized" and the products "banalized", at the cost of quality. Virgil was neither the first nor the last poet to complain that the bread made in big cities had lost its taste. He wondered why it was so different from the bread of his childhood in Mantua, which he ate with *moretum* (translated as "salad" but more like a pesto). In his *Dictionary of Received Ideas*, Gustave Flaubert indignantly wrote: "Nobody knows what filth goes into bread!"

Bread was a staple food; everything else was merely an accompaniment, a *companatico*, as the Romans say. In modern times, the roles have reversed and it is bread that is now more of a side order. Today it allows us to trace a line between the poor and the rich: the former want more bread and the latter are happy to give it up.

II.
TRAILS AND
TRACES

B read followed paths that took it through space and time, memory
and oblivion. It is hard to say where these journeys begin and
where they end. Most often they moved from east to west, following the sun. Sometimes the paths returned the same way, at others they
took a different route, all the while crossing plains, scaling mountains,
roaming deserts. Grain was transported across seas and along rivers
by ship, and on land by carts and packhorses, and even on the shoulders of men and women. Travellers, merchants and caravans all passed
through these crossroads, evoked by prophets, preachers and poets.
Futile though it often is, let us try to imagine what the past was like in
prehistoric times, for memories of those times have been preserved in
stories and legends.

Bread does not travel well: it goes hard, turns stale, becomes rotten.
What does travel well are seeds, customs and the need for this daily
sustenance. Objects, implements and surviving traces attest to the cultivation of grain since preliterate times: grindstones are more durable

than grains; the hoe came before the plough; the mortar is older than the mill and the millstone is contemporaneous with flour. The vestiges of cereals have been preserved in long-extinguished hearths, although the ashes of firewood are similar to the ashes of burnt grains. Rye and barley seem to be more resistant to decomposition than other varieties, whereas wheat is sensitive and quicker to spoil. The various places in which grains were preserved had in common a darkness and silence that helped the seeds to retain their form, if not their fertility. We may never know how long they survived or when they died. The past does not always leave behind a legacy.

Time erases, changes or augments the story.

∽∽∽

Depictions of different grains are found on clay tablets from the ancient cities of Uruk and Ebla, as well as in the ancient Egyptian hieroglyphics of Memphis and Thebes. Mesopotamia was one of the first cultures to sow and harvest grains, and this civilization situated "between two rivers" worshipped Nisaba, the goddess of grain. According to the author of the *Avesta*, the sacred Persian book of wisdom, the goddess' long tresses flowed around her as she walked in the field, amongst the stalks of grain. The book also pays tribute to the stone and iron pestles that crushed the grain for the "offerings of bread"; the water used to make it "rushed down from the top of Hukairya to the Vourukasha sea", spilling into the shimmering sun-drenched fields of Mithra, where golden-hued plants, including the sweet-smelling *hadhanaepata*, were cultivated, in tune with established ritual. Up above, the star Tishtrya shone brightly at night, giving its name to the prophet Zarathustra.

The *Avesta* also tells us the differences between "farmers", "warriors" and "priests", who each had different kinds of bread, from the very best to the most mediocre.

"A bread-offering to all the ancestral gods" was brought to the grave of Gilgamesh, sun of Ninsun. The ferryman Utnapishtim made him "seven celestial loaves" for the afterlife. The *Epic of Gilgamesh*, written in

Akkadian and translated into Hittite, Sumerian and other languages, also celebrated bread.

Thus, perhaps, spake Zarathustra.

Pre-Semitic communities shared similar origins and fates, and more than one particularity differentiated them in the course of their migrations: Sumerians, Babylonians, Canaanites, Assyrians and Syrians, Amorites and Arameans, Akkadians and other peoples of western Asia cited in holy and other books, sometimes drew together and at other times moved apart. Migrating tribes followed various routes to reach the fertile plains bordering the Euphrates and Tigris rivers, while Semitic tribes arrived in Palestine via Suez. Some came through the strait of Bab-el-Mandeb, which was narrower in ancient times than it is today. The names of these people reveal, among other things, their origins: the word Arab most likely comes from *arab'ah*, meaning "desert"; Hebrews, from *ibray* (*ibri*), which means "across", are those who come from the other side of the river, though the name may also come from the verb *habiru* – "to cross". You had to cross the river to reach the fertile grain fields.

Linguists do not agree on the genesis of the first names given to cereals, but they do offer us a chance to establish a link between their interpretations and our suppositions. The names of the first cities and their ruins are often mentioned in tandem with the names of their rulers. Places like Ur, Ugarit, Nineveh, Ashur and Ebla are immediately associated with such figures as the Babylonian kings Hammurabi and Nebuchadnezzar.

In the third and second century BCE, farming and building work such as the world had never seen before – and history has since forgotten – flourished in the "land between two rivers". City and state, literacy and law all came into being at the same time. Legislature and the state protected the production of bread, and the administration and its scribes confirmed its importance, as can be confirmed by the cuneiform clay tablets that they created. King Ashurbanipal had commanded that everything worth remembering be inscribed on the tablets, and the king's order was carried out.

The strange markings conveyed to posterity the first basic knowledge about the art of bread-making. Dagan, the god of grains and fertility, was worshipped from one end of Mesopotamia to the other. His name is associated with the ancient Semitic word *dgn*, which means "wheat". Worshippers prayed to him and brought him sacrificial offerings, and thus emerged the "measure of sacrificial bread". No one knows how many kinds of bread the servants of Assyrian King Ashurnasirpal II served to the ten thousand guests at the banquet he gave to mark the opening of the Palace of Joy, but we do know that the festivities lasted some thirty days.

Bread and its "measure" entered the daily life of the Ancient World.

The cuneiform tablets give, among other things, the names of the cereals. Barley, for instance, is *sheh* (in Akkadian, *sheh*-u), wheat is *ziz* (in Akkadian, *zizu*), spelt is *gig* (in Akkadian, *kibtu*). In the ancient Assyrian language, the word for flour is *tema*. It is not unusual to find drawings that depict ears of grain standing tall, straight, one might even say proud. Some names are easier to figure out than to translate. The Sumerian word *ninda* and its Akkadian synonym *akalu* seem to denote all types of bread. Tablet number XXIII, listed in a glossary known as "Har-ra", names a number of them – more than ten, less than one hundred. They are differentiated by whether they are leavened or unleavened, sweet or savoury, whether they are made with coarse or fine, sieved or wholemeal flour, whether other ingredients have been added such as oil, beer, garlic, onion, herbs, honey, and so on. Coriander and saffron were in the bread served at the table of the king who ruled Mari. Grindstones found next to the ancient Palestinian settlement of Kebara were used to pound wild grains. That was before Semitic tribes crossed Suez and Bab al-Mandaba to settle there.

The title of a handbook composed during the era of the Third Dynasty of Ur (c.2094–c.2047 BCE), could be translated as "Recommendations for the Farmer". When Herodotus passed through these lands, a millennium and a half later, he was amazed to see how fertile they were: "Cereal crops grow so well that a yield of 200 times the weight of the seed grain is not unusual and, when the soil is exceptionally fertile, the yield can increase to 300 times the weight of the seed grain … Blades of wheat and barley grow to a width of at least four fingers."

Despite its rich and fertile soil, Mesopotamia witnessed its own lean years and "lean cows". Inscribed on a clay tablet from the end of the Ugaritic period are the words: "Our land has no more grains."

Archaeology and photography have a grip on the past and the history of ancient Egypt and they won't let go. As for literature on the subject, scholars have done the bulk of the work, for they have discovered and described what Upper and Lower Egypt once looked like, how they united and then separated, what the words "miracle of the Nile" in its Upper and Lower course signified, what damage the river's highest and lowest water levels could cause. Homer admired "the hundred-gated Thebes". The land of the pharaohs venerated the god Osiris, ruler of the underworld, along with the goddess Isis of magic and healing, and their son Horus, ruler of the sky. There are descriptions of the sacrifices offered to them, the rituals honouring them, the celebrations dedicated to them. The hieroglyphics that mention, name and honour them have already been deciphered, and these myths are now an incontrovertible part of history. Bread marks its beginning there, as well as its end: remnants of "ancient Egyptian bread" have been preserved and are exhibited in museums. Various specimens of grain are laid out in boxes and implements are on display behind glass, while the surrounding sculptures and paintings depict scenes of sowing and harvesting, threshing and bread-making or women bending over and pounding the grain or working with the flour. The altar to which the sacrifices were brought resembled a huge millstone. Philology brings to light interesting notions, too, and we see the "The Onomasticon of Amenope" – an ancient Egyptian papyrus that focuses on the New Kingdom and the Eighteenth Dynasty, at one point naming virtually all forms of bread: round, oval, oblong, conical and square, with some loaves even shaped like pyramids.

The generic term for bread was *ta* or *tau*. White bread is *ta hegd*, whereas green bread is *ta uagd*. The latter probably got its name from the herbs added to the dough. During military campaigns, the soldiers were given "Asian bread", which was nourishing and long-lasting. The hieroglyphics also recorded the names *pesen, shenes, nekheru*. Herodotus mentions *kyllestis*, pronounced *keresht* by the Egyptians, and reserved for the common people and slaves. Moulds were discovered for flatbread, different-sized rolls and round cakes, their names teeming with consonants: *bdsh, hts, pzn, dpt*. Although nobody knows how they were pronounced.

Vast fields belonged to the pharaoh. Peasants were given narrow fields to plough. While the baker was respected, he was without much influence. A well-known papyrus speaks well of the baker's work, but not without a touch of irony. "The baker gets on with his work; while he pushes the bread into the oven, his son holds him by the legs; if he slips from the son's grasp, he will fall into the fire." The text also shows that bread ovens were now big enough that a man could push his shoulders through the oven door. In terms of societal organization, paintings and sculptures even depict a scribe checking the sale and distribution of the grains, while we know that farmers paid a kind of tax for a certain amount of grain and workers could receive part of their wages in kind – in bread and beer. Indeed, beer was sometimes seen as liquid bread, since both were made with barley. Presumably, not enough hops grew near the desert!

When it came to cultivation of the land, cows were used to plough the fields, while oxen were kept for a harder job; they helped to transport the stones needed to build the temples, palaces and pyramids. Flooding in the Nile Valley left the soil loose and damp, which meant there was hardly any need for ploughing. As we learn from Herodotus' *Histories*, "when the river [Nile] has come up of itself and watered the fields and after watering has left them again, then each man sows his own field and turns into it swine and when he has trodden the seed into the ground by means of the swine, after that he waits for the harvest; and when he has threshed the corn by means of the swine, then he gathers it in."

Barley was cultivated more than other grains. It was called *it, jt* or *bdt*; and again no one knows exactly how it was pronounced. Hulled barley was different from unhulled barley, and spring barley was different from the winter variety. The *Book of the Dead* states: "I live like grain. I grow like grain. I am grain … I am the owner of bread in Heliopolis, bread of mine is in the sky with Re."

Wheat was called *sut* or *zwt*. Beer was not only a beverage, it was also used as a yeast called *heneket*. Bread flour was also made from lotuses. Herodotus again, that "father of history", was surprised that the Egyptians worked clay with their hands and dough with their feet; he has left us the following story: "When the river has become full and the plains have been flooded, there grow in the water great numbers of lilies, which the Egyptians call lotus; these they cut with a sickle and dry in the sun, and then they pound that which grows in the middle of the lotus and which is like the head of a poppy, and they make of it loaves baked with fire. The root also of this lotus is edible and has a rather sweet taste: it is round in shape and about the size of an apple." These so-called *lotophagi* ("lotus eaters"), were considered more primitive than people who ate bread made with cereals.

Khnumhotep III, a high official in the Twelfth Dynasty who was buried in the necropolis of Senusret III at Dahshur in Lower Egypt between the Siwa and Deir el-Bahariya oases, brought back from the east previously unknown Mesopotamian varieties of grain and bread. Preserved within the walls of the mastaba tomb traces of white wheat and even whiter bread can be found. It was not only the bread that travelled there, it was also the grain.

The long succession of dynasties has left us with so many abandoned or nameless objects, along with those that have obscure or incomprehensible names, with words that change or lose their meaning, and with pictures that fade to the point of almost disappearing. Part of the narrator's work, sometimes the hardest part, is left up to conjecture. The following story, based on verifiable archaeological findings, shows how bread was an inescapable part of everyday life in Egypt: The architect Kha built a tomb in Deir el-Medina to house the mummy of his wife Merit. Next to her dead body he placed more than fifty small loaves of bread for her afterlife. Nowhere else do loaves of bread seem to have been so well preserved or discovered in such number. They can be seen in the museum in Turin, Italy, on the right bank of the River Po. Some of the loaves are lighter than others, almost transparent, like the thin, unleavened flatbreads still made and baked in the south and north of Egypt today. Others are darker, some are carbonized, and others still look just the same as they once did. Most of them are round or triangular, some resemble breasts, others cones. Almost all have a hole in the middle where a leaf, twig or flower can be inserted for taste, fragrance or decoration. Placed around them are wicker baskets and earthen jars, ranging in size from large to small, some no bigger in size than a finger. Scattered everywhere are seeds, the fruits of *doum* palm trees, dates, carobs, onions and cloves of garlic. Little glass bottles and small chests made of sycamore wood hold fragrant ointments and liquids to preserve the beauty of the body that the inconsolable Kha never stopped loving and could not forget. Clean robes lie folded next to sheets and towels. The funerary mask of the dark-skinned Merit is made of linen cartonnage, her shiny eyes of obsidian. She is wearing a lapis lazuli necklace. Everything she could wish for in the afterlife is here beside her; first and foremost, a supply of bread.

An approximately thirteen-metre-long scroll of the *Book of the Dead* lies next to the bread. It contains thirty-three chapters. The hieroglyphics hold a humble and devout message: "O ye who give bread and beer to beneficent souls in the house of Osiris, do ye give bread and beer to me … Let me live on bread of white emmer and beer of the barley … Let me eat under the sycamore tree of Hathor the Sovereign."

To this inscription hanging on the wall of the tomb historians might add, that the architect Kha and his wife lived at the turn of the fifteenth to fourteenth century BCE, or to be more precise during the Eighteenth Dynasty made famous by the pharaohs Amenhotep II and Amenhotep III.

〰〰〰

The climate in Greece is temperate and along the coast it is Mediterranean. Winters are damp but seldom cold, whereas summers are hot and usually dry. To make sure ancient Athens had the grains it needed, its rulers passed laws and adopted measures on their procurement and distribution, and this had an impact on relations between Hellada (Ancient Greece) and the rest of the world. In the region of Attica, the yield was not big enough to feed its people; Attica had to import grain from the fields of

Thessalia, Boetia and the Peloponnese, from Cilicia, and Eubeoa, as well as from the islands of Lemnos and Lesbos. Farmers, either out of need or because ordered to do so, practised crop rotation, keeping some rows fallow, in an effort to extract as much from the land as possible without exhausting it. The historian Xenophon observed that merchants would "sail to wherever they hear there is most of it [grain]; and cross the Aegean, Euxine and Sicilian seas." The quest for the "Golden Fleece" was actually prompted by the Argonauts' desire to discover and exploit, more than gold, the rich granaries of Colchis and the Crimea, where the silt turns the soil dark and gives the land its name *chernozyom*, "black soil".

Let us say that this myth is true; the words of the poet do not dispute it.

Initially, Greek bread was like the kinds offered in Mesopotamia and especially Egypt; there were many sorts, and over the centuries their number grew. We can also find mention of them in literature; in the *Odyssey* the general term for bread is *artos*, while the poet calls round cakes made of coarse and sieved flour *pyrnon*. The food eaten by the poor, which was called *maza*, and was something between mash and a flatbread, predates bread. It's good to see that bakers enjoyed a certain reputation in the Hellenic state. In *Gorgias*, even Plato speaks respectfully of the baker Thearion.

The goddess Demeter, or "Mother Earth", probably came from the east. According to the myth, her parents were Chronos and Rhea and her sisters were Hera and Hestia. She had a daughter, Persephone, with Zeus; and Poseidon, the god of the sea, was her lover – along with, perhaps, the hero Iasion. Distinct from the earth goddess Gaia, Demeter's symbol is an ear of grain and her sphere is agriculture. She was the goddess of harvests long before the Hellenes discovered bread. Myths associated with her name spread far and wide, and poetry was not immune to them. The *Hymn to Demeter*, once attributed to Homer, says: "Happy is he among men on earth who has seen these mysteries."

Demeter was celebrated not only in Eleusis and Athens, but also in Sicily, Crete, the Peloponnese, Thrace, throughout Greece and "Magna Graecia", and all over the Roman Empire. She even eclipsed "Mater Magna" Cybele in Anatolia, and the goddesses Nisaba in Mesopotamia, Thanit in Carthage and Ceres in the Apennines. Surprising her daughter Persephone while she was picking lilies and narcissi, Hades abducted her and carried her off to the Underworld. Beside herself with grief, Demeter donned a mourning robe, lit a torch to light the way and woke up the lions of Etna. She set out to find her child, who was fond of grain fields and affectionately known as Kore. The sun god Helios revealed to Demeter where her daughter was. Furious, Demeter left Olympus, gave up drinking ambrosia, disguised herself as a hunchbacked old woman, and set out for Eleusis. Stopping by a well, she sat down on the "sorrowful stone", and managed to enter the court of King Celeus as a servant, nursing and raising his son Demophon, better known as Triptolemus. But she was soon recognized, and, promising the king's family glory and prosperity, she asked that a temple be built in her honour in Eleusis, by the Virgin's Well, upon the spot where she had earlier met the king's daughter. Nevertheless, she continued to take revenge for the injustice done her. For a long time she forbade any seed to germinate, any ear of grain to grow and any grain to produce a yield.

Even the gods complained that they were being deprived of bread offerings and the first fruits.

Zeus finally dispatched Hermes to the Underworld. The result of his intervention was that Persephone was permitted to spend two-thirds of the year in the light of day, and one-third in the darkness of Hades. Demeter went back to protecting the grains with the help of Triptolemus, the "threefold ploughman", whom she had raised. A bas-relief, probably by Phidias, depicts the two for eternity. The seeds began to germinate again, the ears of grain to grow and the grains produced a yield; famine gave way to prosperity. The tiller's confidence in his plough was restored and he returned to ploughing his furrows. And so people continued to celebrate the goddess of grain not only in Hellada but also well beyond. The temple in Eleusis became the centre of the cult of Demeter and Athens recognized, supported and expanded upon it.

In Agrai, on the outskirts of Athens, the "Lesser Mysteries" of Eleusis took place just before spring, in the month of Anthesterion, whereas the "Greater Mysteries" were in the autumn, in the month of Boedromion.

Women, foreigners and sometimes even slaves were permitted to attend. Pindar wrote that those fortunate enough to have seen these celebrations before dying were "blessed", to which Sophocles added "thrice blessed". No one was allowed to defile the Eleusinian Mysteries. Alcibiades, the famous general and friend of Sophocles, was sentenced to death *in absentia* for having mocked these ceremonies.

The performances turned into secret, mysterious rites, becoming a kind of religion, whose adherents went through a period of initiation before attaining various levels of participation in the secrets of the mysteries. The festivities were held for more than 1,000 years and in the centre of it all was Demeter, a sheaf of wheat around her brow or on her shoulder, a poppy or narcissus sometimes in her hand, and accompanied by a crane, her bird of choice. The Akkadian town of Phygalia, perched on a steep cliff overlooking the Neda River, celebrated Black Demeter, the fearful avenger.

This myth, which may well predate bread, helped to turn bread into a myth of its own.

During the days of celebration, loaves of different sizes were brought in a special "basket", to be served together with the drink *kykeon*, made of barley flour, mint leaves and red wine. A number of Roman emperors, from Augustus to Marcus Aurelius, were, to varying degrees, part of the Eleusinian Mysteries. The emperor Claudius planned to move the Demeter festivities to the banks of the Tiber, in the Eternal City.

Thus, the mysteries became reality and that reality became history.

These rites were held continually until the fourth century CE, when the emperor Theodosius banned them as being alien to nascent Christianity. St. Clement of Alexandria attacked the pagan heresy practised in Eleusis, accusing it of refusing to accept the Eucharist. The Eleusinian temple was not spared even by the Goths in their move to destroy the Roman Empire, which had spread to Hellenic and Egyptian territory in the early fourth century CE. Their leader Alaric, making a dignified entrance into Eleusis in a white *chlamys* or cloak, asked the actors to perform Aeschylus' *The Persians*. He wept as he watched. Meanwhile, according to the records, the Gothic barbarians desecrated the inside of the temple, smashing statues, carrying off gold chalices and cups in feedbags, seizing silver trays on which bread and wine had once been served. Cries of *Christus panis!* echoed all around.

Christianity was to replace the myth of Demeter, the Mass the Eleusinian rites and the Eucharist the "Mysteries".

Feasts and *symposions* were always part and parcel of the Lesser and Greater Eleusinian Mysteries. A Hellenic banquet, known as a *deipnon*, had to have the best food and drink, and the finest breads. These were occasions to discuss *polis* and politics, the sciences and the arts, to recite poetry, sing and dance, to make music and perhaps even love with a young *epheboi*. The *symposiarch* was there to maintain the dignity of the gathering and mitigate the effects of the jugs of wine. Participants were divided into the good (*agathoi*), those who drank moderately, and the bad (*kakoi*), those who became inebriated.

Bread was a mediator.

The literary or cultural genre of the banquet or symposium – if one can talk about their genre – can be found in the works of Plato and Xenophon, Plutarch, Macrobius and many other classical authors. The writings of Athenaios, a Greek born in Egypt, in Naukratis, near Hellenized Alexandria in the third century CE, have helped us to learn more about the atmosphere at these events. Indeed, he seems to have read many of the books stocked in the famous library of Alexandria. As soon as he moved to Rome, he became a favourite guest of the patrician Publius Livius Larencis during the reign of Marcus Aurelius. Endowed with an extraordinary memory, but not with literary talent, Athenaios compiled a monumental collection called *Deipnosophistae* ("Sophists at the Symposium"). The compilation runs to several volumes and includes valuable information about the consumption and variety of bread. There is so much of it, in fact, that for this occasion it might be best to resort to the literary methods known in Formalism as montage and citation in order to present them, that is to listing facts and quotes and summarizing them according to need and purpose:

Monuments to Demeter were built in several places in Boeotia; they were called *megartos* ("big loaves") and *megalomazos* ("huge round cakes", *maza*); in Sicily Demeter was called *Himalis* (Protectress of the Grindstone); in Delos, her cult was celebrated at the *Megalartria*, or "festival of the big loaves". In his *Gastronomy*, Archestratos writes: "first the gifts of fair-haired Demeter shall I call to mind" (all these quotes are taken from Athenaios' aforementioned collection). For the Thesmophoria festivities in Syracuse, sweet breads made of sesame and honey were dedicated to the goddess Demeter and her daughter Persephone. Their round shape was reminiscent of a woman's pubic mound, and they were ambiguously called *mylloi* (most likely from the word *mylla* – mouth). *Zymites*, says Athenaios, is leavened. Different kinds of round cakes made of unsieved flour were called *semidalites* and *chondrites*; those made of unsifted flour were called *synkomistos*. In his *Protochre*, the poet Antidotus mentions "bread baked on burning embers" – *escharites*; in *Ganymede*, the playwright Eubulus praised "twice-baked bread" – *dipyron*; Athenaios notes that the poet Alcman liked a pepper-bread known as *makonides*. The bread *obelias* owes its name to the fact that "in Alexandria it was bought for one *obol*". *Atabyrites* is bread from Atabyria, as mentioned by Sopater in *The Women of Cnidus*. *Laganon* is easy to digest but is not nourishing says Aristophanes in his play *Assemblywomen*. Apollodorus of Athens notes that breadcrumbs are called *psothia* by some and *attaragoi* by others. In his dramas, Epicharmus lists various kinds of bread, such as *homoros*, *staitites*, *enkris* and *hemiartion*, to which Sophocles added *orindes*, rice-bread made "with seeds from Ethiopia", and a flatbread called *plakitas*. The Ionians called their bread *knestos*, the Eleans called it *bacchylos* and Hecataeus and Herodotus mentioned the Greek bread *kyllestis*. The best bakers were the Phoenicians, Lydians and, along with them, the "newcomer Cappadocians". This banquet of bread – like our much shorter montage from Athenaios' list – closes with the words of the celebrated physician Galen of Pergamon (129–c.200 CE): "We shall not eat until you have heard me say what the descendants of Asclepius have written about the different kinds of bread." Remember, he was speaking in Rome, in the patrician home of Larensis, where Athenaios was a welcome guest. Visitors were probably served *garum*, instead of the Greek *kikeon*. We are told that after the meal, the banquet continued late into the night with a "discussion about salty fish".

Although extensive, Athenaios' compilation does not mention certain details that we might like him to have included. For instance, other sources mention *enkryphias*, which was baked on hot stones and covered with ashes; *aphtopyres* baked on hot coal; *obalies* baked between two plates of iron; *kribanites* or *klibanitos* made in a clay or metal dish; *lekythites*, where the dough is mixed with oil; and *destreptities*, where it is mixed with oil and milk and pepper. The first cake was sweetened with honey and in Hellada was called *melitates*. When wine was added it was called *ortoyolanos*.

We may know that Sophocles liked the bread of Ethiopia, but we do not know how it made it to the shores of Greece from the desert of Africa; was it by land and sea, in caravans or on boats? Aristophanes extolled a white bread called *amilois*, which he tasted in the home of the wealthy Athenian Demias. Having gained a certain fame at banquets or *symposions*, poets were welcome guests in the palaces of both aristocrats and tyrants. Anakreon was hosted by Polycrates, the tyrant of Samos. Aeschylus and Simonides found refuge in Syracuse, in the palace of Hieron I. The Macedonian Antigone hosted the poet Antagoras of Rhodes. Guests were obliged to dedicate a verse or two to their host, an exercise at which Pindar excelled. Going further back in history, there is no evidence that Homer or Hesiod frequented the tables of the powerful, and Xenophon complained that the winners of sports competitions were celebrated more than were poets, protesting: "My knowledge is more valuable than the brute strength of certain people or horses."

Chrysippus of Tyana compiled a book about the art of bread-making called *Artopoikon*. Since the title is a composite of the word *artos* ("bread") and a derivation of *poeio* ("I do", "I make", sharing the same root with the word for poetry), it could be freely translated as "the poetics of bread". Unfortunately, only a few excerpts, known mostly through second-hand sources, have survived. The author claimed that there were seventy-two different kinds of bread in Hellada.

Catalogues like this usually mention the odd cake, as well.

There are many comparisons and metaphors in classical works that are linked to grain and bread. Homer depicts his heroes and their exploits not only at sea but also on the threshing floor and in the granary: "As winds in sacred floors chaff lifteth ... and gold-tress'd bright Demeter separates with strong winds' breath the husk and grain ... so white a-top with dust th' Achaeans grew, which th' horses' feet upcast to th' brazen sky..."; "... as one who yokes broad-browed oxen that they may tread barley in a threshing-floor ... even so did the horses of Achilles trample on the shields and bodies of the slain." In Sophocles' *Antigone*, the chorus extols the work of the "plough". Science and art stand side by side in the secrets of the Sieve of Eratosthenes, that simple and ancient algorithm used to find the prime numbers up to any given limit. Xenophon did not like brown flour and Demosthenes loathed millet. It was not just farmers and botanists who spoke about mildew on the grain – both Plato and Aristotle used it as a metaphor. The "bread of slavery" appears in Aeschylus' *Agamemnon* and in *Enquiry into Plants* Theophrastus reminds the reader that the first period of the sowing season coincides with the setting of the Pleiades.

In the second century CE, Artemidorus of Daldis in Lydia, also known as Artemidorus of Ephesus, visited various Asian, African, Greek and Roman provinces. He recorded and interpreted the dreams of his contemporaries in his *Oneirocriticon* ("The Interpretation of Dreams"), distinguishing between two main types of dreams: *enumpnion* – wishful thinking; and *oneiros* – a prophetic dream. He was particularly interested in bread. If we dream we are eating an ordinary loaf of bread, that, he says, is a "good omen", but if a poor man dreams of "white bread", reserved for the rich, he may fall ill. It is best to dream about barley bread because it is food "sent to human beings by the gods". Dreams about granaries and silos can bode both well and not so well – if we see these structures "in a dilapidated condition" then it will be the latter. Grain, the harvest, the granary and bread itself entered dreams that were good and transparent and dreams that were bad and murky. You who dream, do not forget Artemidorus.

The Roman story of bread seems less complicated than the Hellenic – though it, too, has its colourful moments. Bread was baked in Rome much later than in Athens, and therefore the cult of the goddess Ceres is considerably younger than that of Demeter. The Hellenic goddess bequeathed her Roman counterpart the sheaf of wheat around her brow, but not her crane. And while the homages paid to her in Latium were more modest than the "mysteries" of Eleusis, they were sometimes more festive.

For a long time, the Romans ate a kind of porridge called *puls*. Pliny the Elder writes: *pulte non pane vivesse longo tempore Romanos.* That seems to refer to a kind of mixture of spelt or bean flour. In Old Latin the word *far* denoted all types of grain, and is probably related to words like *har* in Egypt or *bar* in Palestine – we know that the names of bread often travel with it, sometimes ahead of it, at others in its wake. Generally speaking, in Romance languages the word for flour – *farina* – stems from the same root. For a long time, the Romans boiled or fried their grains and it was evident that their precursors, the Etruscans, knew more about baking than their invaders and masters. Making their way from Anatolia in what were probably prehistoric times, the Etruscans had the opportunity to learn how the peoples they encountered made bread.

Everybody learns from others, although we do not always know who these "others" were or why they were designated as such.

There are times when the history of Rome coincides with the history of bread. Memories of famine, want and epidemics haunted the city like a ghost. In the second century BCE, the Gracchi brothers – politicians Tiberius and Gaius – attempted to introduce reforms in Roman society that would reduce the differences between rich and poor. They used legal provisions to limit the size of large property holdings and the incomes they brought in. It was not easy to make people accept this goal. Bread played an important, sometimes even a decisive role here. The owners of great landed estates did not hesitate to destroy the harvest of anyone who refused to cede their land to them. "At night your lean oxen and famished horses … will be sent among your neighbour's green corn, nor will they be led home from thence before all the new crops go into their own ravenous bellies," wrote the incorruptible Juvenal. Grains were imported from Sicily and Tunisia; almost a third came from Egypt by boats that sailed between Cyrenaica and Ostia.

Rome was not yet Rome, but it was soon to become an empire, instilling pride in its citizens and fear in the rest of the world.

It was a long time before the porridge that early Romans ate became flatbread and round cake, and then finally both turned into real bread. According to legend, Roman soldiers threw hard bread rolls at the Gauls setting siege to the Capitol, to show them that they had enough food to withstand any onslaught. There is also the story of the playwright Plautus, whose name is associated with the millstone. Having spent everything he had on his passion for the theatre, he was compelled to turn a millstone like a slave just in order to survive. This experience was the inspiration for three of his comedies, one of which is called *Enslaved for Debt* (*Addictus*). By then flour-milling was far from unknown in the Eternal City; indeed, it was considered to be one of the most difficult of jobs. But the city, *urbs*, only learnt about the wide variety of bread that existed when Roman legions captured Macedonia in 146 BCE. Roman citizens – *Quirites* – were astonished to discover the richness and choice of bread in the Hellenic province they had just captured. It probably did not boast the seventy-two different kinds of bread that Chrysippus of Tyana claimed, but it certainly had more than anywhere else.

Rome may have lagged behind in some areas at times, but it quickly caught up and overtook its rivals. Many Greek bakers were taken prisoner during the capture of Macedonia, with many carried away to work in the Roman capital. There were so many, in fact, that for a while the word *Graecus* was a synonym for *pistor* – baker. Along with the different kinds of bread adopted from Hellada, new varieties, with descriptive names, kept emerging in the city itself and the number of bakeries mushroomed.

The common people were entitled – with a special permit (*tessera*) – to a plain bread called *panis civilis*. Caesar, in his palace, was served *panis palatius*. Soldiers were given *panis castrensis*, sailors *panis nauticus*, plebeians *panis plebeius*, peasants *panis rusticus*, slaves *panis sordidus*. *Panis siligineus*, made with the finest wheat flour, called *siligo*, was held in high regard. Juvenal describes a bread that was soft and white as snow, made with the very best grain (*sed tener et niveus molliqne siligine factus*). The poet Horace extols the delicious bread he tasted at the table of Maecenas, while the ladies of the house tended to their complexion by rubbing their face with *madidus*, the moistened soft centre of the bread. We do not know anything about the *panis Picentinus* and *panis Alexandrinus* mentioned in the *Apicius*, a collection of Roman cookery recipes compiled in the first century CE. In Pompeii, some loaves escaped the lava and ashes that followed the eruption of Mount Vesuvius. They can be seen near the millstone and bread oven depicted on a fresco that was spared by the tragedy. On the terraces of the Colosseum, *panis gradilis* was distributed to the people for free. That is probably what inspired Juvenal to write in his Tenth Satire a phrase that was to be remembered for centuries to come: *panem et circenses* – "bread and games".

Roman poets reached for comparisons and metaphors that usually had more to do with the land that produced the grain than with the sea crossed to transport it. In the *Aeneid*, Virgil compares navigation to tillage: *maris aequor arandum* ("the sea must be ploughed"). In the *Georgics*, however, he ignores the oar and sail in favour of the plough and ploughshare: "Now to tell the sturdy rustics' weapons, what they are, without which neither can be sown or reared the fruits of the harvest; first the bent ploughshare and heavy timber ... Well, I wot, he serves the fields who with his harrow breaks the sluggish clods and hurdles osier-twined hales o'er them; from the far Olympian height him golden Ceres not in vain regards ... O happy farmers, too happy should they but know their blessings!"

State policy on grains in the Roman Empire – *annona*, from the word *annus* (year) – was entrusted to the magistrates, chosen from among the *aediles*, and regulated by the legislators. Its orientation was decided by the emperor, and slaves bore the brunt of it. In the spring, the capital became the stage for festivals known as *cerealia* that celebrated Ceres. New mills sprouted up on the outskirts of the city. Sieves were made out of thin twigs, and sometimes parchment imported from Egypt. Farmers would let the land lie fallow and practise crop rotation to preserve the fertility of the fields and meadows. The number of bakeries grew: during the golden age of the empire, there were more than 300 in the city. The poet Martial complained that he couldn't sleep from the racket they made. Colourful ceremonies dedicated to Fornax, the goddess of the bread oven, were known as *fornacalia*.

Bakers began to organize themselves into guilds – for example, the *corpus pistorum* and the *collegium silaginariorum* – supported and helped by the authorities. Emperor Trajan issued a decree saying that any foreigner who worked as a baker and baked enough measures of bread over a period of three consecutive years, could enjoy the same rights as a Roman citizen: *jus Quiritinium*. Even after the division of the empire, the Theodosian Code protected the orphans of bakers: *qui in parvula aetatem relinquitur*.

Treatises both wise and practical were devoted to agriculture, among them the writings of Marcus Porcius, better known as Cato the Elder, who wrote *De Agricultura*, and Lucius Columella (*De re rustica*). Columella attempts to explain why his compatriots, taught how to cultivate the land by the gods themselves, were obliged to import grain from overseas provinces so as not starve to death. By the great gate of Rome, still known as the *Porta maggiore*, a mausoleum was built to the baker Marcus Vergilius Eurysaces, who rests there beside his aides and young wife. The graceful, sensuous figure of a female baker thus enters the collective European imagination, her shoulders and breasts covered with a white tunic.

Lack of bread brought into question a ruler's competence and reputation. In Rome, the emperors wore a crown made of sheaves of wheat, like the goddess Demeter or Ceres. At the height of the Roman Empire, the ills of the past finally seemed to have been overcome and one could believe that the famines of yore would never happen again. Unfortunately, that was not to be so. While on the one side Christianity was gaining in reach and strength, Caesar was losing power. Finally, the Eastern Roman Empire and the Western Roman Empire separated in 395 CE and confronted one another. Byzantium gained its freedom and forged its power, taking control of the routes that led to the grain-rich regions on the islands and in Anatolia. Over time, it became increasingly dangerous to sail to the shores of Africa and the markets of Cyrenaica and Carthage, with their surrounding grain-rich fields. By the mid-fifth century CE, riding at the head of hordes of Huns, Attila cracked his whip and instilled fear. The barbarians, who ate gruel and raw meat, demolished city ramparts and seized the surrounding fields. When Alaric, king of the Visigoths, besieged the capital, its population was half of what it had been in Augustus' day. The Christians' compassion for the poor had its limits. None of St. Paul's disciples were wealthy. Lean years followed and soon all sorts of diseases re-emerged. In its twilight days, the empire was no longer strong enough to ensure that each of its citizens had a ration of bread. *Annona* had failed. Rome foundered, among other reasons, for lack of grain.

The Middle Ages, with its black bread, fasting and penitence, was approaching.

༽༽༼

According to ancient legends and lore, there were nine Arab tribes, the descendants of Iram, son of Sam, grandson of Nuh/Noah, and of Ismail/Ishmael the firstborn of Ibrahim (Abraham). They hailed from Jazirat al-Arab ("Island of the Arabs"). Desert nomads gravitated northwards towards Syria and Palestine, Sinai and the Red Sea. In the south, they moved to the grain-rich Yemen, which, together with the surrounding region, was known by the mythic name *Arabia felix*. In the plains of the "Fertile Crescent", Arabs learnt more about crop-growing and irrigation, along with new ways to prepare food and drink. The first caravans are mentioned in Assyrian chronicles that date back more than 1,000 years before Islamization. In the battle of Qarqar (853 BCE), the Arab king Gindibu, also known as Jundub, came with his army and camels to the aid of the Aramean king Abad-Idri of Damascus, the biblical Bar-Hadad. The tribes moved out in different directions, towards Palmyra and Aleppo, Damascus, Basra and Alexandria. Some made their way south to Mecca and Aden. They carried grain seeds, spices, fragrances, frankincense, balsam, cinnamon, nutmeg, myrrh, cassia, aloe and many, many other things still unknown to these lands. The desert, drought and hunger propelled the newcomers to seek out regions endowed with springs, fields and pasture ground. On their long and arduous journey, the Arabs came to learn about different grains and the production of bread, adopting and adapting them to their own taste and needs.

These crossroads resonated with the words of the first prophets, in anticipation of the true, most important prophet of all.

"And there entered the prison with him (Yusuf) two youths. Said one of them, 'I dreamt that I was pressing grapes (*hamr*). Said the other, 'I dreamt that I was carrying on my head loaves of bread (*khubz*), that birds were eating of. Tell us its interpretation; we see that thou art of the good-doers.' This is the only mention of bread in the Quran. Muhammad the emissary and messenger ate dates. The famous *ajwa* (or *ajwah*) dates flourished in his native town of Mecca and in the "lighted city" of Yathrib, which was to become Medina (*el-Medinetu-l-'Munawwera*). "He who eats seven ajwah dates every morning, will not be affected by poison or magic on the day he eats them," wrote the Persian scholar al Bukhari. The Islamic scholar Ibn Omer (Umar) quotes the words of Muhammad: "Amongst the trees, there is a tree, the leaves of which do not fall and so is like a Muslim ... the date-palm tree." Its roots are deep and strong. In spite of drought, it manages, sometimes in the middle of the desert, to produce a sweet and nourishing fruit. Dates have different names in different regions, sometimes *t'mar*, or *tafezuin* or nakhila, while it is also known as *deglet-nour* – "date-palm of light".

Unlike Judaism or Christianity, Islam does not give bread a special place in its liturgy. It was consecrated by those who needed it most: the family and the Muslim community – *ummah*. The Quran mentions neither the sieve nor the plough, but it does speak of grain: "We have sent down blessed rain from the sky and made grow thereby gardens and grain from the harvest ... We split the earth in fragments, and therein cause the grain to grow ... It is Allah who causes the seed-grain and the fruit-stone to split and sprout."

And the surah "Yasin" says: "We give life to the dead earth and bring forth from it grain."

The canonical importance of the *hadiths*, the sayings of the Prophet Muhammad, is acknowledged – they serve to complement the Quran. In a region that boasted the best palm trees and was most wanting in grain, those who conveyed the words of the Prophet had good reason not to mention the word bread in vain. Nevertheless, Salih-al-Bukhari maintained that Muhammad liked barley bread, and recommended it to the sick and ailing. Muhammad's daughter Fatima offered her father a piece of that same barley bread. Imam Ahmed, who heard and recorded Muhammad's reply, quoted him as saying: "This is the first food your father has eaten for three days." According to the *hadith* left for posterity by the Persian Abu Dawud: "For the Prophet Muhammad vinegar was the best condiment for bread". Al Bukhari quotes Abu Hazim as saying that the Messenger of Allah never saw a sieve in his house. The question is: would he have had a chance to see one in a region overflowing with palm trees, rich in dates, but where grains were rare?

Islam brought the Arab tribes together and attempted to unite them. It created religious services and supported state institutions. The great Umayyad and Abassid caliphates came into being. Tribes set out, side by side, for new regions; they subjugated Egypt, conquered the Mashreq and Magreb regions, and reached the coast of Sicily. They crossed the Strait of Gibraltar, naming it after their commander Jabal-al-Tariq, and marched into Spain, came to Portugal – and stopped when they reached the Atlantic. The conquerors could now behold the achievements of ancient cultures. Alexandria – Iskanderia – once one of the capitals of the Mediterranean, knew about Egyptian and Greek and Roman bread, and perhaps even some others. Tunisia had preserved the traditions of the Phoenicians, well versed in the art of baking, as well as those of the nimble Carthaginians who worshipped Tanit, the goddess of fertility, and of the Romans themselves who ruled a sizeable part of Africa. The Berbers knew about bread before the arrival of the Arabs. The Sicilians had adopted the rite of the Eucharist before Islam ever reached their shores. The Spaniards and the Portuguese knew about not only Christian rites, but also about Jewish ones: unleavened flatbread, unleavened and leavened loaves, *matzah* and *chametz*.

Grains and their yield were often linked to the stars and their brightness. There was even an age-old belief that grain grew faster at night than during the day. Sowers and reapers would gaze at the starry sky and observe the phases of the moon. Perhaps the symbol of a young moon with a star in the middle evokes the times when men worked the fields at night rather than in the unbearable heat of the day. The Prophet did not mention this symbol, which is older than the Islamic faith, but the Shahada was on the first flags, and in some countries it serves as a coat of arms to this day. It is inscribed in Arabic calligraphy on a black background: *La ilaha illellah Muhammadun rasulu llah* ("There is no deity except God, Muhammad is the messenger of God").

In the vast expanses conquered by the Arabs before their clashes with the Mongols and Turks there were many names for bread. *Khubz* is the most widespread, sometimes referring to food in general. In Egypt the word is *aish*, which also means life. Its literary name *serid* is less frequently used. In Morocco, the word *taboon* denotes a woman's pubic mound, but in Tunisia it is a small, round, puffy bread; the similarity between its form and name is no coincidence. Berbers call their bread *adjeroom*, probably a deformation of the Latin *agrum*. *Regif* is a flat round bread and *'adjin* the dough used to make different kinds of bread. The famous travel writer Ibn Battuta (1304–1368) heard that the people of Isfahan used the Persian words *nan* or *nanna* for bread, especially when talking to children. He noted that when walking across Syria on foot, he had passed by gardens, with palm-groves both to the right and left protecting passers-by from the sun, with merchants sitting in the shade of the trees, selling bread and dates.

This is a region where shade promises relief, pleasure, even perhaps happiness.

Who knows how many varieties of bread were made by Arab bakers, and especially women: *khubzu-l-'mellah*, baked under hot ashes, dating from ancient times and similar to the bread mentioned in the Old Testament; *khubzu-l-'huwara*, white bread made from wheat kernels; *khubzu-l-'semiz*, bread made with fine flour, known as *semiz* or *semid* for short; *khubzu-l-'hushqar*, an inexpensive, simple bread made with wholemeal flour, destined for the market and souk, and therefore often called *khubzu-es-suk*; the more highly regarded sesame bread, whose "gold nuggets" found a place in the verse of Ibn Haddad-Hussein, the seventeenth-century Yemini Islamic scholar. The root of many surnames comes from the word for baker – *habbaz*. Records mention bread made of lentils, poppy seeds, acorns, beans, carobs, chickpeas, dry figs, ground dates and a mixture of seeds: "One can like everything in this world, but no one can resist grained bread", wrote the poet Al Mamouni, while the Arab prose writer el-Gahiz, in his *Kitab a-Bukhala* ("The Book of Misers"), says that bread is "the king of all foods".

Generally speaking, nomads had a harder time of it than settlers, as did farmers compared to merchants and Bedouins compared to townsfolk. There is no wood in the desert to make a fire, and not even enough camel dung for fuel. Those with experience will know how to find an unusual plant that grows in the sand; called *halfa* grass, it ignites quickly and burns for a long time. They say that before placing the dough on the hot stone, one should first roast a leg of goat on it to give the bread taste. The Bedouins put the leftovers of their meal, especially bread, beside the tobacco, salt and tea in their leather saddlebags. The smells do not compete with each other, but rather inexplicably merge into one, and Bedouin bags retain this smell even when empty.

Along the coast of the African continent, and especially inland, we find the nomadic Tuaregs. Their language is closer to Berber than Arabic, but they all share the same religion, Islam. Among them, I witnessed how the women, of a darker complexion and wearing blue or red scarves, let the men tend to the bread and the goats or mouflons that sometimes follow the caravans. Our guide translated a desert song for us, part of which goes: "Give me a camel, a saddle and a tent, and I will be a happy man."

Notions of happiness in the desert differ from those elsewhere, and the same is true of attitudes to flatbread' – they are not the same everywhere.

In the provinces the Arabs occupied, the authorities passed laws and decrees on bread and grain and oversaw their procurement, distribution and consumption. Within the space of several centuries, a number of important culinary books appeared, including *Kitab al tabikh fi-l-Magrib wa-l-Andalus fi 'asr al-Muwahhidin* ("The Book of Cooking"), written by an anonymous author who lived at the time of the twelfth-century Almohad dynasty, *Adab-es-sufra* ("Table Manners") by al Sindhi bin Muhammad and *Risalet fil-ihtirami-al-khubz*) ("A Discussion on Respecting Bread"), written several centuries later by the wise Abdul Ghanī al-Nābuls.

When Sufism appeared in the eighth century CE, it began defining and spreading its own notions of life, food and conduct. Sufis preferred vegetables and fruit to meat, and bread itself to everything else. They wore humble woollen cloaks, from which they probably got their name: in Arabic *suf* means wool. Their mystic view of the world and the universe tried not to betray the surahs of the Quran. Rather than become a sect or heretic, they strove to remain simply the embodiment of their faith and religious enthusiasm, considering themselves to be "the poor before God" (*fuqara ila Allah*). Although Islam does not encourage monasticism, *tariqats* were similar to monasteries. And they always served good bread ahead of the humble meal. Dervishes (from the Persian *darvish*, mendicant) gathered in brotherhoods. They ate and debated together in a way that was somewhat reminiscent of Hellenic banquets, though in many respects it was also unique to itself. "The whirling dervishes aspired through their movements and dance to attain perfect ecstasy," observed one of their admirers who wished to remain anonymous, not out of fear but out of modesty.

The Persian poet Mevlana Jalaluddin Rumi came in the thirteenth century from faraway Afghanistan to the town of Konya, which at the time was Persian; today it is in Turkey. It is here that the Sufi tradition of *mevlevis* was born and here that Rumi wrote the *Mathnawi*, a work that is at the same time lyrical, epic, narrative and poetic. Fragments from the extensive poem are read aloud to the sound of a reed flute called the *sema*. Under the almost untranslatable title *Fihi-ma fihi* ("It Is What It Is"), we read: "Someone who hasn't eaten for ten days and another who has eaten five times a day – they both see a loaf of bread. The full one sees only more food, but the hungry person sees life itself." In the poems of his *Divan-e Shams-e Tabrizi*, Rumi returns to bread: "If it is bread that you seek, you shall have bread ... Let the lover hungry for bread dream away ... O life of my life, not for bread alone do we come here ... The light of the moon enters this mill, before it returns to the moon, we are near the place where bread is offered."

Rumi elevates bread to the heights of the moonlight, but does not forget to warn, as did Christ, that one cannot live by bread alone.

In old Cordoba, on the banks of the Guadalquivir, there was a bakers' quarter known in Arabic as *Rabad ar-rakkakin*. It was said that this was where the best bread in Andalusia could be found. It was near a "sweet basil shop", *khavanit ar-reihan*, just a few steps away from the "garden of wonders", *Munjet al-adjab*. Cordobans came here to get good bread. Before tasting it, they would first wash their hands and rinse their mouths with fresh water at one of the surrounding fountains. They did not cut the bread with a knife, rather they tore off pieces, eating them one by one. During the reign of the Umayyads, Cordoba numbered some twenty quarters along the banks of its great river before it was destroyed in the month of *shawwal* in the year 633 of the Hijri (1236 CE). The bakers' quarter was famous, and everyone knew about it and that the way to enter was through the gate of Saragossa, *bab Saraqusta*. Ebu-l-Walid Muhammad ibn Ahmed Muhammad ibn Rushd walked the streets: "it would take a hundred years for that long name to become Averroes", twentieth-century author Jorge Luis Borges remarked in his short story "The Aleph". He reminded us that the philosopher's ancestors had come from the dry deserts of Arabia, and therefore liked to listen to the gurgling sound of water, especially when it came from a fountain in a hidden courtyard. Averroes knew about the neighbouring bakeries, where another frequenter was Ha-Rav Moshe ben Maimon, better known as Maimonides. This Jewish philosopher and physician, a native of Cordoba, wrote *Commentary on the Mishnah* in Arabic. In times of yore, the legends of Arabs and Jews, both Semites, converged around a loaf of bread. Cordoba was a prime example of this; perhaps that is why it was destroyed.

The thin, almost translucent flatbread survived all through times of destruction and exile. It lived on in the Moroccan side of the Mediterranean, in Tétouan. Thousands of exiles of Arab origin, known as Moriscos, sought refuge here, along with a fair number of Sephardic Jews. Tétouan is called the "odalisque of Andalusia", a beauty "reposing in a bed of flowers", its face covered in "the white burnous of the Prophet". Around the Casbah one can still see the remains of the ancient ramparts, Spanish in construction, Mudejar in style. Here, as in Cordoba, you can enter from various sides, through gates bearing old names like *Bab Mqabar, Bab Saida, Bab Remuz, Bab Nuader*. No other city, except perhaps Fez, has preserved so many Andalusian features. At the souk *Ghars al-kabir*, one can find all kinds of bread, unleavened round cake, flatbread, flat soft rolls, rolled-out sheets of dough. Some say that you won't find anything better anywhere.

That was certainly true of the bread in Cordoba before the last Moriscos and Sephardim left.

Ancient and modern times crossed and clashed in Upper Egypt. The return of a fair number of Arabs from the Iberian coast and plains, following the Reconquista, saw the emergence of the "silk sieve" (*manhol harir*), the "fine silk sieve" (*manhol harir na'em*), the "bran sieve" (*manhol selk*), the rye sifter and the wheat sifter (*gorbal*), as well as a special small sack made of palm leaves (*goffa*), used to carry fresh bread.

In his famous book *Muqaddimah*, ("Prolegomena"), the historian Ibn Khaldun summarized, among other things, what was known about agriculture. In his native Tunis, he lived under the rule of the Hafsid dynasty; in Morocco he discovered what life was like in both the palaces and prisons of the Marinid dynasty; in Egypt he witnessed the rule of the Mamluks; in Grenada he met the Nasrid sultan; in Cairo he taught at Al-Azhar University; in Damascus he conversed with Tamerlane. None of his Arab contemporaries could match his experience. Writing in a style that was both simple and persuasive, he cautioned that the cultivation of cereals and foodstuffs depended on the procedures and means that stimulated and made them possible. "The fruit of this craft (agriculture) is the obtainment of foodstuffs and grains of agriculture to produce grain and food – and for that one needs not only to till, sow and oversee the soil, harvest the ears of grain, thresh and extract the grain from it…" Because even the simplest meal "requires utensils and tools, that can be provided only with the help of three crafts … the crafts of the blacksmith, the carpenter and the potter." Ibn Khaldun also tried to explain the Prophet's attitude to the plough and the way certain *hadiths* talk about it. He presumed that the Messenger of Allah despised the plough not as an instrument of labour, but rather as an instrument that was sometimes used to exploit poor labourers.

The author of *Muqaddimah* compares leaven with a talisman, saying that it is like yeast (*hamira*), composed of the same elements of earth, water, air and fire. In its essence and form, leaven is capable of changing whatever substance it enters. It can be likened to an elixir (*el-iksir* in Arabic), he says.

Bread has forged many trails, old and new, past and present. There is not enough space in either history or a story to evoke them all. Those who depart on a journey and those who return seldom eat the same bread.

III.
FAITH AND
BELIEFS

B read is present in religion and prayer. The Judaeo-Christian tradition introduced it into its rites and liturgy. Before or at the same time as the Torah and Bible, it was sanctified by the myths of Babylon and Mesopotamia, and by the rites of the Near and Far East. It is mentioned in the Quran and eulogized in the *hadiths*.

Sometimes bread and religion follow the same, close, parallel paths. And where they diverge, we find discord, disputes and conflicts.

When Adam and Eve were cast out of the Garden of Eden, the Almighty pronounced the following sentence: "In the sweat of they face thou shalt eat bread, till thou return unto the ground; for out of it wast thou taken; for dust thou art, and unto dust shalt thou return." Hunger and destitution drove the Israelite nomads to Egypt before they ever kneaded their bread. They became slaves of the pharaohs, working in the fields and stables, building fortresses and towns, erecting Pi-Ramesses and Pithom. The life of the Egyptians themselves was not without its trials and tribulations either. Their harvests were often lost or wiped out, destroyed by hail and lightning, drought and floods, the excessively high or excessively low water levels of the Nile, the winds blowing in from Ethiopia, driving swarms of locusts ahead of them. During lean years, the newcomers were the poorest fed. Their emaciated, tortured faces appear on the bas-reliefs of the Old Kingdom and the frescoes of Khnumhotep. Troubled nocturnal dreams plagued not only the neglected exiles, but the rich local inhabitants, as well. Scribes recorded and tried to interpret them, and at such time soothsayers and sorcerers became advisors to the rulers.

Abandoned by his family and expelled to Egypt, the young Joseph distinguished himself with his talent and wisdom. He became an aide to the Pharaoh and donned the kind of woollen tunic worn by dignitaries. During the drought and famine in Canaan, he sent to his father Jacob and his brothers ten donkeys and ten jennies laden with grain.

The huge numbers of Israeli refugees living on the banks of the Nile troubled the pharaoh. He ordered their newborns to be drowned. A little boy, placed in a wicker basket and entrusted to the waters of the river, was saved. That little boy was Moses. He learnt to read and write hieroglyphics. Yahweh had chosen him to save his people and lead them back to the Promised Land, to the slopes of Mount Sinai. Despite the resistance and incomprehension he sometimes encountered among his compatriots, the prophet announced the end of slavery and prepared for the Exodus. Fleeing the pharaoh's army, which was at their heels, the Israelites carried with them bread dough that, in their haste, they had not managed to leaven.

Thus was born the rite of "unleavened bread".

The Old Testament Book of Exodus reads: "And Moses said unto the people, Remember this day, in which ye came out from Egypt, out of the house of bondage; for by strength of hand the Lord brought you out from this place: there shall no leavened bread be eaten. This day came ye out in the month of Abib." (*Abib* means young barley). "Seven days thou shalt eat unleavened bread, and on the seventh day shall be a feast to the Lord … and there shall no leavened bread be seen with thee, neither shall there be leaven seen with thee in all thy quarters … This is done because of that which the Lord did unto me when I came forth out of Egypt."

There were already two main words for bread in the Hebrew language: *lehem* and *pat*. Flatbread baked on hot stone and sprinkled with ash was at the time called *ugah* in Hebrew.

The journey across the desert was long and arduous. Moses led the exhausted people, protected during the day by the clouds, and guided at night by the torchlight. They reached the Red Sea. Its waters parted, say the Scriptures, allowing the exiles to cross to the other shore. And then, in a huge wave, they closed again, drowning their pursuers.

There are shallow waters and marshes along the banks of the Bitter Lake, between El Qantara and Suez, that probably could have been crossed on foot, but that does not take away from the significance of this biblical scene.

The people wandering in the desert could not appease their hunger. Their patience waned, their memories surged. There was a time, after all, when in the land of Egypt "we did eat bread to the full". Yahweh decided to come to the aid of the desperate people. "And it came to pass that at even the quails came up and covered the camp; and in the morning the dew lay round about the host. And when the dew that lay was gone up, behold, upon the face of the wilderness there lay a small round thing, as small as the hoar frost on the ground. And when the children of Israel saw it they said one to another: It is manna; for they wist not what it was. And Moses said unto them: This is the bread which the Lord hath given you to eat. This is the thing which the Lord hath commanded, Gather of it every man according to his eating, an *omer* for every man according to the number of your persons; take ye every man for them which are in his tents." Anything taken beyond the designated measure was infested with worms – that was the punishment meted out to the greedy and grabbing. The word *manna* comes from *man hu* ("what is it?"). Some claim that one can still see a similar phenomenon on Mount Sinai. There is a type of tamarisk that secretes a translucent liquid that congeals and hardens during the cold desert nights. It is sweet and the Bedouins delight in this gift of the desert.

The nomads call it *man* in their dialect even today.

The biblical scene unfolds in tandem with fateful events and parables: the exodus from Egypt, the arrival in Canaan, the burning bush, the Golden Calf, the Ten Commandments, Moses on Mount Sinai, construction of the Tent of the Congregation, the establishment of feasts, including the feast of "unleavened bread". Bread is mentioned and celebrated in both the Old Testament and the New, and in the Jerusalem and Babylonian Talmud. To commemorate the exodus from Egypt and liberation from slavery, the Torah prescribes eating only unleavened bread for Passover (*Pesach*), and removing or destroying all trace of leaven from the home during the days of Passover. *Matzah* (*matsah*) is unleavened bread, *chametz* is not. *Challah* (*hallah*) has several meanings: usually it is a white, special bread twist prepared for *shabbat*, the seventh day of the week, and major Jewish holidays. It is linked to the old tradition of offerings – a piece of dough is tossed into the hot bread oven, known since ancient times in Mesopotamia and Babylon as a *tannur*.

To make each of these breads one of the five major grains was chosen: wheat, barley, rye, oat or spelt.

When making *matzah*, it was important not to let any flour come into contact with water, out of fear that the dough might start to ferment. To prepare the *shmurah matzah* for *seder*, says the *Halakhah*, the grain must be dried before being ground or even right after harvesting. This custom is a reminder of both the poverty of slavery and liberation after the exodus. The Pesach *Haggadah* notes that "This is the bread of affliction that our fathers ate in the land of Egypt."

Clear, vivid instructions and advice are also to be found regarding bread in the Babylonian Talmud: "Our Rabbis have taught: Four things are said concerning bread – we may not place raw meat upon bread; we may not pass a cup full of wine over bread; we may not throw bread; we may not rest a dish upon bread…" But there are also some words of caution: "The one who is about to break bread is not permitted to do so before salt or relish is placed before each one at table … If a man wishes to avoid stomach trouble, he should dip bread in wine or vinegar summer and winter … In the rich house of rav Chisda (a Jewish Talmudist who lived in Kafri, Babylonia in the early fourth century CE), bread made with the best grain was given to the dogs, which did not seek it; while in the house of the poor Rabbah, barley bread, when there was any, was given to the household."

This advice is given in the holy Hebrew books. The Babylonian Talmud is better preserved than the Jerusalem Talmud, which is partly destroyed. In the Old Testament, the Second Book of Kings mentions a man who came from Baal-Shalisha, bringing "twenty loaves of barley and fresh ears of grain in his sack ..." With it the prophet Elijah, Eliyahu in Hebrew, fed a hundred hungry people: "and they ate and had some left over". This *multiplication of loaves* precedes that in the New Testament, and in hagiographies.

The Haggadah, with its knowledge of bread, sometimes served as a model or inspiration for storytellers. Philo of Alexandria, known as Philo Judaeus, whose work brings together the Hebrew tradition, the *logos* of Greek philosophy and the Christian heralding of the "contemplative life", wrote a treatise called *De agricultura*. He speaks sympathetically about the life of the "therapeutes" who ate unleavened flatbread, poured water over it, sang as one and prayed aloud.

Feast days were an occasion to offer different kinds of bread. For Easter (*Pesach*), in the month of *nisan*, at the start of spring, *matzah* bread was usually served, accompanied by bitter herbs and wine. That was when, following the "order" established by tradition and known as *seder*, enlightening chapters were read out from the Haggadah. *Sukkot*, celebrated at the beginning of autumn, after the harvest, in the month of *tishrei*, recalls the "huts" used by the Jewish people for shelter as they crossed the desert. For this occasion, "four species" are carried: three twigs from the myrtle tree, two from the willow tree, one from the date-palm tree and the fruit of a citron tree. In the same month, *Rosh Hashanah* marks the start of the New Year, with prayers to Yahweh to inscribe the faithful in "the Book of Life". This celebration is also known as *Yom Teruah*, the day of shouting or "blasting", because Moses ordered that the *shofar*, a ram's horn, be blown. *Yom Kippur*, the Day of Atonement, starts with a fast and ends with a feast. *Hanukkah*, celebrated at the beginning of winter, at the end of the month of *kislev* and the start of the month of *tevet*, commemorates the liberation of the land of Israel from the Greek conqueror Antiochus IV of the Seleucid dynasty. That is when the flickering light of the *menorahs* illuminates the world around them.

Each of these days of commemoration and hope was accompanied by a particular type of bread, honouring tradition and affirming one's faith.

The Jews faced many an adversity that made their position precarious both in and beyond their land: their expulsion from Jerusalem, the destruction of the Temple, their dispersion in the diaspora, the emergence and sudden expansion of Christianity. Centuries would pass before the worshippers of Yahweh received, first orally and then in writing, the messages of the Kabbalah and of *The Book of Splendour* – *Sefer ha-Zohar*. The author of the book, written in archaic Aramaic at the end of the thirteenth century CE, had to hide his real name, presenting his work as a Talmudic commentary that was more than 1,000 years old. His name was Moses de Leon, he lived in Spain and was close to both the Kabbalists and the Gnostics. Well versed in the Talmud and the related treatises of Judaic theology, he decided to give a new interpretation of the Pentateuch.

Moses de Leon's poetic praise of bread was worthy of the Psalms: "When He gave the Torah to Israel, He gave them to taste of that supernal bread of the Tree of Life (Malkuth) ... Matzah is indeed the fruit of the Tree of Life ... By means of this bread, the sons of Israel were enabled to perceive and penetrate into the mysteries of the Torah and to walk the straight path ... The Zohar holds that matzah is the bread of faith ... It is the bread that inspires faith ... Partaking of it instils in us peace ... Rabbi Akiva takes the phrase *lebem ahhirim* to mean 'bread that the ministering angels eat'. The Zohar accepts this and sees manna as the gift of God ... The Scriptures say: And Reuben went in the days of wheat harvest, and found mandrakes in the field ... The Zohar adds: on Rosh Hashanah, New Year's Day is a day of judgement for those who have not accepted the healing food, and have neglected the medicine, that medicine being matzah ... Chametz is the evil impulse ... There is no bread outside of the Torah."

In the *Zohar*, lines imbued with the spirit of the Kabbalah are devoted to the waters and their colours present in unleavened and leavened bread. "In space there are forty-five divisions, each of which is distinguished by different colours. The seven colours of the white light penetrate the seven abysses, and by the effect of their vibrations upon the rocks therein, cause the water to flow forth. This water inundates the abyss ... All the lights meet at one point. Light, darkness and water blend and from this mixture are born invisible, crepuscular shadows..."

What will bread made with such water be like? What colour crust will it have? Who will eat it? These are among the questions that form part of the story of bread.

The expulsion of the Jews from Spain and Portugal starts less than 200 years after the appearance of the *Zohar*, almost at the same time as Christopher Columbus' ships set sail across the ocean. Some of the Jews professed conversion to Christianity in the hope that it would save them. They were dubbed *Marranos*, which meant "swine" in Spanish and Portuguese. Secretly, however, they continued to practise their traditions and tried to preserve the faith of their ancestors. They went to great lengths to save their *matzah*, *chametz* and *challa*, but they also remembered the lechem and *pat* and even the still older kind of bread known as *ugah*.

Bread kept alive their sense of self-awareness and belonging.

Dispersed all over Europe and the Mediterranean, the Jews brought their customs and traditions to the different countries in which they eventually settled. There they helped to make bread better and more appreciated. It arrived as far as Bosnia, near the Sarajevo synagogue, at the foot of Mount Trebević. In places, it is still called *patišpanj* (in other words *pan di Spagna*).

In Thessaloniki, and in Smyrna, and in Constantinople, this same bread was served at the tables of Sephardic families with respectful humility.

◊◊◊

Christianity adopted some of the Hebraic breads and related traditions. The words of the Old Testament became an integral part of Christian learning, and the New Testament elaborated upon or reinterpreted them. Even so, they retain their original meaning. A major innovation came with the *Eucharist*, giving thanks and mercy, based on the blessings of bread.

Having first been rejected and persecuted, the Christian faith came to introduce new prayers and rites, other images and parables. But it did not give up the "showbreads" that had once been presented on the specially dedicated table in the Temple, although they now had a different meaning: the twelve loaves no longer represented the twelve tribes of Israel, nor was "bread of the first fruits" abandoned, but it was interpreted differently. "Breaking bread" – *fractio panis* in Latin, *krasis artou* in Greek – also acquired a new meaning. The old models of "hospitality" and of "giving" were preserved, as well. Those from whom God withheld his mercy continued to eat, as is written in the old psalms, the "bread of tears", "bread of sorrows" and "bread of ashes". Sinners were left with the "bread of lies", and the lazy with the "bread of idleness".

The rupture brought about by the word of Christ was first expressed in the New Testament, with its new images, notions, teachings: the crucifixion and resurrection of the Son of God, the issue of his mother Mary's immaculate conception; the Holy Family and its flight to escape the massacre ordered by Herod; the twelve apostles reunited at the Last Supper; the miracle of the "multiplication" of the loaves and fish; the transformation of water into wine. The evangelists recorded and passed on to coming generations the words of Christ: "I am the bread of life. He that cometh to me shall never hunger ... This is the bread which cometh down from heaven, that a man may eat thereof and not die ... I am the living bread which came down from heaven; if any man eat of this bread he shall live for ever ... Your fathers did eat manna in the wilderness and are dead ... Verily, verily, I say unto you, Moses gave you not that bread from heaven; but my Father giveth you the true bread from heaven, for the bread of God is he which cometh down from heaven and giveth life unto the world." St. John the Evangelist remembered and passed on his words, and here noted the rejection of Moses' bread as a gift from heaven, offered in the form of manna, which reflects the break between Judaism and Christianity.

Noting Christ's gesture, St. Luke recorded: "And he took the bread and gave thanks and brake it, and gave unto them saying, This is my body which is given for you: this do in remembrance of me." This scene is confirmed by St. Matthew the Evangelist. St. Mark added: "Take heed,

beware of the leaven of the Pharisees, and of the leaven of Herod ..."
And St. Matthew said: "beware of the leaven of the Pharisees and the
Sadducees."

According to a legend that is not part of the biblical canon, Jesus'
mother Mary attended the school of the prophetess Sibyl for a while.
She took a piece of leavened bread that the prophetess had thrown way,
placed it under her armpit and took it to her mother Hannah, the future
St. Anne. Thus was formed the hollow of the human armpit. And ever
since, leaven has helped Christian bread to rise, swell and become soft.
The story, which for a long time circulated among countries stretching
from Jerusalem to Rome, is still remembered, but appealing as it is, it has
not been accepted as gospel.

St. Paul started off as a fierce opponent of this new faith of Christianity,
only to become its most ardent advocate and make a huge contribution.
Born in Tarsus, in Cilicia, this tireless traveller and preacher interpreted
and developed Christian teaching, completing a part of the work that the
apostles had left unfinished and the first councils had not even begun.
His conversion on the road to Damascus offered a fascinating example
of revelation and he contributed, among other things, to the reverence
for bread.

The circumstances that trace the path he followed and this eventful
experience deserve mention.

Paul, whose Hebrew name was Saul, was travelling to Damascus with
a caravan, hoping to avoid the dangers faced by any lone traveller at the
time. He spoke to no one, knowing that the Nabateans did not like the
Israelites and that therefore it was better for him not to reveal that he was
a Jew. Walking from the desert of Judea towards the oasis of Jericho, the
only food he had with him was unleavened bread and onions. Growing
in the Jordan Valley were trees with dates so succulent that they were as
good as cakes. Having had his fill, he continued on his way and stopped
in Hippos, by the Sea of Galilee, where they made tasty soft-crusted
unleavened bread. He took some as provisions for the coming days and
put them in his sack.

Crossing the Golan Heights was exhausting. His eyes were drawn to the peaks of Mounts Meron and Hermon, and the sight of them lifted and inspired him. When Christ appeared before him in the Hauran Valley, St. Paul was struck blind by the light he emanated. He soon regained his sight, perhaps by applying pieces of warm bread to his eyelids, as was recommended by the ancient healers of the day. To be honest, descriptions of the "road to Damascus" rarely mention the bread that on that trip provided nourishment to Saul-Paul, the saint and convert. We do not know if, on the way, he had stopped in the towns of Kanatha and Sweida to obtain fresh provisions of bread. He was hurrying towards the riverbed of the Barada, whose waters feed the surrounding oases and the city of Damascus. This ancient city, at the intersection of routes to Anatolia, Arabia and Mesopotamia that led down to Jerusalem and continued across the sea all the way to Delos, was exposed to Hellenic influences and tended to observe pagan customs. These were not propitious conditions for Christian preaching. The future saint had to earn a living, so he started making waxed canvas flaps for tents, then tying them together and stretching them. His hands and fingers became so calloused that, as he himself admitted, he was only able to write in large script. He rubbed the palms of his hands with dough mixed with water from the Barada River, which was considered to have curative properties. He probably used this same dough to make the bread he ate.

For all the many hypotheses linked to the road to Damascus, the only sure thing is the journey itself.

After the appearance of Christ, St. Paul was to make increasing reference to bread and its divine nature when preaching the word of God: "Is not the bread that we break a participation in the body of Christ ... Because there is one loaf, we the many are one body, for we all partake of the one loaf ... Whosoever shall eat this bread and drink this cup of the Lord unworthily, shall be guilty of the body and blood of the Lord."

A descendent of the Israelites and renegade of the Hebrew faith, the Christian saint inherited from his ancestors a certain reserve when it came to leaven. Addressing the Corinthians, he advised them: "Let us keep the

feast, not with old leaven, neither with the leaven of malice and wicked-
ness, but with the unleavened bread of sincerity and truth ... Purge out
the old leaven."

Confrontations and conflicts with other religions such as Arianism, Mani-
chaeism, Mithraism, the Monophysites and Gnostics, with the still
embedded Hebraic tradition and Hellenic mythology, with heresies of
different origins and apocrypha from various sources, all posed a chal-
lenge to Christianity, opening it up to all sorts of trials and tribulations.
Only time came to decide which doctrine was to be acknowledged the-
ologically, which teaching was to be declared *orthodox* teaching. This
presumed the rejection of all the conflicting theses and unsubstantiated
writings that were circulating from Anatolia to the shores of the eastern
Mediterranean, and was the duty of the Church councils and the Fathers
of the Church in the centuries following the death of Christ. One of the
first and most important such councils was held in Antioch on the left
bank of the Oronte River, at the foot of Mounts Sylpius and Stauris, in
a Roman province exposed to the influences of Judaism and Hellenism.
It was also home to one of the biggest libraries in the world, comparable
to those in Alexandria and Pergamum, and had welcomed a number of
saints such as Paul and Peter, Barnabas and Jean Chrysostom.

It was in Antioch that the word "Christian" was spoken for the first
time. And it was also here that dignitaries of the Church, representa-
tives and interpreters of Christianity in the East, assembled in an effort
to resolve some of the many unanswered questions. It was during this
period that Constantine was to proclaim Christianity the official religion,
capable of not only uniting the Church but also of strengthening the
empire that it ruled. Among other councils that took place was the one in
325 CE in the city of Nicaea, on the eastern banks of the mysterious Lake
Ascanius, whose waters are green in one place and purple in another, a
city that lies at an important crossroads that leads to the hinterland and
sea, Anatolia and the ports of the Mediterranean. Ephesus, near the Sea of
Marmara, which like a mirror reflected the city's resplendent architecture,
also hosted an important council. The fourth ecumenical council, held in

the fifth century after the birth of Christ in the town of Chalcedon, in the province of Bithniya, is remembered for condemning the heresy of the Monophysitism, with the presence of Roman Emperor Marcian lending an official stamp of approval to the condemnation.

On a number of occasions, important decisions were taken in the majestic city of Constantinople, which was eventually to become the centre of the Christian East. These large meetings do not seem to have concerned themselves with bread as such. Long debates were held on the liturgy and its order, on the relationship between the Son of God and his Father, which was considered "consubstantial" (*homousios*), on the Eucharist and its meaning, and on the "epiclesis" – invoking the Holy Spirit whose presence transmutes bread and wine into the body and blood of Christ. Written records were seldom kept at the time and the oral tradition failed to preserve many of the details, consigning them to oblivion. Fortunately, St. Clement of Alexandria preserved a few important phrases for posterity:

"Wine is to bread what the contemplative life and gnosis are to the active life and everyday faith ... Blessed are they who give bread to those that hunger after righteousness."

Over time, the *Acts of the Apostles* were gradually replaced by the apologies of the martyrs. The Hebrew language of the Old Testament was often supplanted by Aramaic and its Syrian dialect. The Bible's translation into Greek – the famous *Septuagint* – is considered exemplary but it did not include the New Testament. The inroads made by Christian piety in a world marked by Greek, Roman, Persian and other pagan traditions, became increasingly tangible. Christianity was "Byzantinized" before it was "Latinized". It used images that Hebraic tradition had once banned. Bread acquired a growing, visible importance. The New Testament set for it a new scene, one that was full of events, morals and allegories such as the "strait gate", "lost sheep", the condemnation of the Pharisees and the expulsion of "the merchants from the Temple", the "healing" of the sick, the prayer at the Mount of Olives, Gethsemane, the Last Supper, Golgotha, the crucifixion, the resurrection and the encounter with the disciples on the road to Emmaus after the resurrection. Christian teaching brought to light new, previously unknown symbols and parables – the basket and platter, among other things, recalling the "multiplication" of loaves and fish.

The name of the small town of Bethlehem, where Christ was born, is a composite of the Aramaic words *beth* (house) and *lehem* (bread), although other etymological interpretations are possible. In the Lord's Prayer, the main prayer of Christianity, linguists discovered certain differences between what Matthew says and what Luke says: the one speaks of "bread for the coming day" whereas the other talks about "bread for each day". Perhaps the Aramaic word *maar* (tomorrow), translated into Greek with the adjective *epiousios*, gives it a clearer eschatological meaning, one that St. Jerome's Vulgate did not adopt.

Etymologies often conceal stories known to them alone.

Christian monasticism spread and from the outset it had two aspects to it: one was eremitic, close to the desert (*eremos* in Greek), and the other cenobitic, open to communal life. Different rules of fasting are defined and described in the Old and New testaments, the Talmud and the Bible. Bread is present in almost every one of them.

Fasting encourages the spirit to oppose the domination of the body. It helps us to purify ourselves, to free ourselves from greed, to merit God's forgiveness and mercy. Moses, as Christ himself later did, spent forty days in the desert, in "a land not sown" as the prophet Jeremiah put it. They set an encouraging example for asceticism. The Great Fast, or Lent, lasts forty days. The Christian calendar was to mark other days of fasting, as well, days when black bread, dry and rough, made of barley, rye and sometimes oat, was eaten more than white bread made of wheat. Amongst the early Christians, there were those who mortified themselves so severely that their face and body, sometimes even their spirit, looked utterly exhausted, at times even deformed. Indeed, it was from the word Christian that the word *cretin* (*cretino* in Italian, *crétin* in French) evolved.

The true disciples of Christ believed that to boast about or make a show of fasting lessened its value.

There were more differences than similarities between the Christian agapes and Greek *symposions*. At the same time, they tried to perpetuate the memory of the Last Supper and Eucharist and to promote charity. "Our agapes feed the poor", declared St. Cyril of Alexandria. They were held in the evening – *post lumina*, writes Tertullian, and different kinds of leavened and unleavened bread were brought out onto the table, then broken and distributed to the assembled faithful. They drank wine, red like the blood of Christ, though sometimes also white. One of the frescoes in the ancient *Capella greca* in the cemetery of St. Priscilla in Rome shows the guests for the agape assembled around loaves of bread, wine, fish and a sacrificed lamb. The rite of communion was sometimes performed before and sometimes after dinner, and was not regular. Sources rarely mention the discussions or appropriate songs that animated the Hellenic *symposions*. All the same, paganism entered, or better said reappeared, in the agapes, divesting them of some of their ritual solemnity. Immoderate drinking and eating, sometimes even lust, meant moving away from faith and prayer. St. Paul cautioned: "Now in this that I declare unto you I praise you not, that ye come together not for the better, but for the worse…. When ye come together therefore into one place, this is not to eat the Lord's supper." The councils held in Carthage and Laodicea at the end of the fourth century would forbid Christians from organizing and attending such gatherings. Apparently, however, this ban failed to achieve the desired result and had to be reasserted at the succeeding councils of Orleans and Tours. For some celebrations, bread was made in the shape of a human body, but the Church disapproved of that, as well. On the other hand, the agapes sometimes had the character of funeral repasts, like the ones held in pre-Christian times, and on such occasions there was a special "bread for the dead".

In some regions this custom survived for a long time and even today has not been universally abandoned.

If myth and prophecies predominate in the Old Testament, revelation and preaching have a bigger presence in the New Testament. The works of the Fathers of the Church bring together theology and homilies. A similar evolution is evident with regard to bread, which no longer falls from heaven like manna, and is made with and without leaven. Christianity sanctified bread: blessed, broken, shared.

Church teachings tried to reduce or efface the differences that appeared between oral legends and written legends, to compose and adjust rites in keeping with the demands of the Christian faith. The history of the Church recognizes eight great "doctors" (teachers): four Greek Fathers and saints – Athanasius, Basil, John Chrysostom and Gregory of Nazianzus, and four other saints and Latin Fathers – Ambrose, Augustine, Jerome and Gregory the Great. First and foremost of the fifty-odd Fathers of the Church were Tertullian and Cyprian, both born in Carthage, Irenaeus from Anatolia, probably born in Smyrna, Origen of Alexandria, Ephrem the Syrian, Isidore of Seville. In their sermons they all celebrate bread as the body of the Saviour. According to Irenaeus, the Eucharist is contrary to Gnosticism, which is overly given to analysis. Cyprian sees believers in the Eucharist as "the union of many grains" in one bread. For Origen, bread is the salvation of the world (*panis pro mundi salute*) and therefore he who brings it to the people daily should be honoured. More frequently and with greater detail than the other Fathers, Tertullian interpreted the meaning of the Eucharist bread: "Christ says 'I have desired (*con concupiscentia*) to eat this Passover with you' because it is not worthy of God to desire a body other than one's own … When he said "this is my body", he was thinking of the form (*figura*) of his body, but it could only be a form if it was a real body, because something that is empty is but an illusion (*phantasma*) and could not have a form." This Church Father rejected the interpretation that later emerged among Christians, which said that the twelve loaves of presentation represented the twelve apostles, not the twelve tribes of Israel. For this and other character traits Tertullian was considered as hard "as a diamond" (*adamantios*).

Isidore of Seville observes that "bread is served with all food" and therefore everyone "craves it". The author of *Etymologies* cannot resist his passion for and habit of studying and mentioning names and origins. He says that *panis cibarius* is not refined (*nec delicatus*) and was given to slaves. He distinguishes between bread that is unleavened – *azymus*;

slightly leavened – *acrozymus*; and even less leavened – *acroaymus*. But he does not ignore the other kinds of bread that were known at the time on the Christianized shores and in the towns of Spain, especially Seville, breads like *spungia panis* (sponge bread), *subcinericius* (cooked on hot embers), *focacius* (hearth bread). Writing about the word bread – *panis* – the etymologist adds that in Greek *pan* means "all" (*pan enim Graece omne dicitur*), although the origin of the two words is not the same. We are also beholden to the venerable exegete St. Jerome for translating the old names of bread. According to John Chrysostom, the Eucharist is forever and is never exhausted: the body of the Lord is not under, not with and not in place of bread; it is bread itself.

St. Augustine, too, often celebrates bread. In his *Confessions*, he comments on the Psalms: "Christ says, 'I am the living bread, which came down from heaven' … Christ, eternal and daily bread, gives strength to the martyrs. When we explain the Scriptures, we, so to speak, break bread. I have broken bread for you – that is what I have just presented to you. The bread of angels is the Lord who has become man. Thou light of my heart, Thou bread of my inmost soul, Thou power who givest vigour to my mind, who quickenest my thoughts…" The scenes depicted by Augustine, writer and saint, evoke the seed, wheat, grain, chaff, sieve. "Be good with wheat. Too much chaff is on the threshing floor, but when it passes through the sieve, it will separate … What is more minute than grains of wheat? Yet they fill the barns … Pass human acts through the sieve, refute my words if I am wrong."

Stories spontaneously leap off the pages, summarizing the history of bread. In retracing its history, St. Augustine also preaches: "The earth bringeth forth grass, that it may bring forth bread from the earth. What earth bringeth forth grass? Pious holy nations. That bread may be brought forth out of what earth? The word of God out of the Apostles."

In Christian thought, at the altar, in religious rites and theological discussions, bread becomes ever more present and visible from one century to the next: communion, the Eucharist Host and monstrance, the tabernacle, the chalice, the Eucharistic transubstantiation and consubstantiation of bread and wine into the body and blood of Christ, bread as the word of the Lord, the *logos* of faith, the symbol of the sacrament.

St. Thomas Aquinas would sing of "the bread of angels":

Ecce panis angelorum! / Factus cibus viatorum. / Vere panis filiorum.

"Behold, the bread of angels is made the food of pilgrims; truly it is the bread of the children."

The Church and its faithful named St. Honore the patron saint of bakers, and St. Michael the guardian of granaries and silos.

∞∞∞

Many parts of the apocrypha, rejected or condemned by a Church seeking to establish the unity of the faith, speak of bread. They mention the multiplication, breaking and sharing of bread by adopting, completing or variously interpreting sections of the Old and New Testament. They especially cite the Last Supper and its consequences, Jesus' retreat to the desert where Satan urged him to turn stones into bread, the wedding feast at Cana, Jesus praying on the Mount of Olives, the crucifixion, the resurrection, the repast at Emmaus and again bread, broken and shared there. The texts that were proclaimed apocryphal were not fabricated, but the official stand taken by the Church, based on the first councils, considered them unacceptable, especially those parts with gnostic roots. The religion denied notions that diverged from its own, the catechism rejected them, the faith proscribed them, the dogma refuted them. Canonized texts gained orthodoxy. Heterodoxy became heresy.

And yet, bread and its identification with the body of Christ were seldom disputed.

The Gospel of Judas is one of the most contested amongst Christians, like Judas Iscariot himself. The manuscript, translated into Coptic, was discovered in Egypt in 2006, where for centuries it had laid buried in a tomb not far from the village of Maghagha, near the banks of the River Nile. What makes it different from the canonized Gospels is its strongly gnostic overtones. Still, it was known to exist because it was the subject of condemnation by Irenaeus, bishop of Lyons, and Clement of Alexandria, who not only dubbed it heretical, but also accused it of "Cainism". The manuscript depicts Judas not as a paid traitor but as Christ's closest disciple, who penetrated His secret and His truth more deeply than any of the others. At the very outset, the text depicts the ritual of the Eucharist in an unusual manner: "One day He [Christ] was with his disciples in Judea … When He found them gathered together and seated and offering a prayer of thanksgiving over the bread, [He] laughed. The disciples said to [Him], 'Master, why are you laughing at [our] prayer of thanksgiving? We have done what is right.' He answered and said to them, 'I am not laughing at you. You are not doing this because of your own will but because it is through this that your God [shall be] praised." Christ laughs or smiles three times in this apocryphal text. Reading the text in the Sahadic Coptic dialect into which it was translated, probably from Greek or Aramaic, it is difficult to tell whether he is laughing or merely smiling. The Gospel according to Judas does not mention bread as the "body of Christ", but it does say, in a manner similar to Matthew, Mark and Luke, that "it is impossible to sow seed on the rock and harvest its fruit".

Most of the other apocrypha are less heretical or disputable when it comes to bread. In *The Martyrdom of St. Bartholomew,* the saint repeats the Old Testament saying that "man shall not live by bread alone, but by every word that proceedeth out of the mouth of God". According to the Acts of the Apostles, during his stay in Rome St. Paul refused to give communion to the adulterous Rufina. A raggedly dressed little boy brings St. Peter a piece of "rye bread", the kind that was made in the Eternal City. *The Acts of Barnabas* mentions that in Antioch St. Paul, although wracked with illness, still managed to eat bread. St. Jude Thaddaeus, brother of James the Less and patron saint of desperate cases and lost causes, (Thaddaeus means "stout-hearted" in Aramaic), baptized Princess Sandokht: "He blessed the bread and gave it to her and those with her," whereupon she distributed the bread to the faithful. *The History of Joseph the Carpenter,* again rejected by the Church Fathers, says that upon his return from a long journey, St. Joseph found Mary to be three months pregnant; surprised and distressed, for days he did not eat, not even bread for comfort. *The Book of Elchasai* revelations speak out against

"Greek bread", intended for the tables of the rich, while The *Life of Andrew* depicts the future saint Nicholas as an aging old man, living only on bread and water. In *The Gospel of Nicodemus*, Pilate mentions the feast of unleavened bread (*Hag ha-mazzot*), an old Jewish ritual. The *Book of the Rooster* invites the apostle John to partake of "bread dipped in wine". In the *Homily on the Life of Jesus and His Love for the Apostles*, also apocryphal, Christ warns his disciples that any among them to whom he has not offered bread with his own hands is not worthy of sharing his body.

Speaking to the dying Christ on the cross, it is said that Joseph of Arimathea sighed: "Those whom you fed with bread should now come to your aid."

If bread is often mentioned in the apocrypha, it is seldom the reason the works were proscribed. Other motives were at play, and other consequences at work. The apocryphal gospels were written in various languages: in Aramaic, Christ's mother tongue, more often in Greek and Latin, but also in Ethiopian, Coptic and Syrian. Each is marked by traditions of its own, adding something here, taking away something there, each in its way influenced Church teaching. A life of Jesus, written in Arabic, is known by the title *The Arabic Infancy Gospel*. Whatever their genre, all the apocrypha speak respectfully of bread: in the *Apochryphon of James* (aka "The Secret Book of James") brother of John, and those of Matthew, Simon and Bartholomew; in the *Apocalypse of Paul* and those of Peter, John or Thomas, Sidrach and Esdras; at the beginning and end of the *Sibylline Oracles* and in several passages of the *Doctrine of Addai the Apostle*. Their teachings are closely linked to the circumstances in which they emerged. One new faith was being propagated, while an older pagan one was still extant. Some biographies became hagiographies, some stories legends, some sermons stories and some stories preaching. The theological centres of Rome and Constantinople were stricter than the congregations and monasteries in the provinces. The *Gospel according to St. Peter* was discovered in Egypt in 1866, in the grave of an ordinary Byzantine monk, while *The Apocalypse of Peter* (*apokalypsis*) survived only in its Ethiopian version. Bishops proved to be more intransigent than the simple monks in accepting all works. Apocryphal writings competed with patristic texts.

After resolving their differences with them, the works of the Fathers of the Church became a part of history and thereby immutable.

In the first centuries after the crucifixion of Christ, there were numberless apocrypha in the East and in Byzantium; by the Middle Ages they had proliferated in Western Europe, too. On both sides, they strove to conform to theological and popular views, and sometimes to literary views, as well. Some were based on gnostic doubt, others inclined more towards an esoteric inspiration, and others still – especially in the East – held close to the Kabbalah. The Reformation would be less strict in its reading of these texts. Painters and sculptors found subjects for their frescoes, icons and mosaics in apocryphal motifs.

Dante seems to have been very familiar with the apocryphal *Apocalypse of Paul*, which describes the torment of hell in detail. It inspired him when writing *The Divine Comedy*.

Apocrypha lean more towards dispute than discussion. Nevertheless, some of them manage to reconcile wisdom and faith. *The Acts of Philip* teaches us that we must be in harmony with ourselves in order to be worthy of the bread about whose glorious secret we have heard: According to an anonymous comment, this secret would find a home inside us and gradually tame us until it made us complete in both body and spirit.

The quest for the Holy Grail is also based on an apocryphal story. This identified the Grail as the chalice in which wine was served at the Last Supper and in which Joseph of Arimathea collected the blood of the Son of God, stabbed by the lance of a Roman soldier. Knights and the faithful embarked on a quest to find it. For centuries, the Order of Malta and the Templars searched for the Holy Grail and its secret in sanctuaries and monasteries. It fascinated both poets and painters in the Middle Ages, inspired the "Breton cycle" in literature and provided material for *Perceval, the Story of the Grail*. Once again blood and wine were united in legend. Bread, too, stood on equal ground with the cross and the chalice, often in the form of the Host.

∞∞∞

After the end of World War II, in the ruins of Qumran (Khirbet Qumran of old) by the Dead Sea, which at this spot drops more than 100 yards below the sea level of the Mediterranean, scrolls written in Hebrew and Aramaic were found. The exciting discovery aroused the interest of theologians and the faithful. At first the story sounded like a fable that one might call *The Wolf and the Lamb*. The lamb strayed from the flock out towards the desert and the Bedouins went to look for it. One of them, named Wolf (*Dhib* in Arabic) of the *Ta'amnireh* tribe, crept into the nearest cave, crawled to the back and suddenly found himself looking at an array of clay pots, the kind once used to hold and carry grains, oil and wine. But there was not a trace of either grain or oil or wine inside them. Instead, they contained yellowing sheets of parchment and papyrus, rolled up in linen cloth. The shepherd told his tribesmen what he had found. They looked around for more caves and were rewarded for their effort. They then began to sell the unusual manuscripts in the surrounding towns, especially in Bethlehem. News of the discovery spread far and wide. Experts showed up and saw for themselves the exceptional nature of the find, which only pushed up the price of the scrolls even further. Eleven such caves were discovered. Each was numbered according to the order in which it was found: Cave 1, the biggest, then Cave 2, and so on up to the last one, Cave 11. One of the manuscripts was etched on copper foil, which had escaped corrosion. Several short fragments were written in Greek. This proved to be one of the biggest archaeological finds of our age.

The scrolls were ascribed to the Essenes, a religious brotherhood who lived in the region. They "live west of the Dead Sea ... without any women ... without money; with only palm branches for company", wrote Pliny the Elder, adding: "Below used to be the town of Engaddi." The sect diverged from Judaic orthodoxy, and in the first and second centuries BCE, it preached a teaching close to Christ's. Theological disputes over the relationship between Essenism and Christianity continue to this day.

Fragments of the scrolls, parts of which were crumbling and rotting, the writing effaced, were reconstructed into pieces of varying size. They repeatedly mentioned bread which, in a way, is a link between the traditions of the Old Testament and the New: "The vision [of bread] has made heavy my eyelids," we read in one of the manuscripts ... "Every small measure of seed sown shall give a multitude of measures." The central figure in the scroll called *Community Rule*, discovered in the first and most important of the eleven caves, is The Teacher of Righteousness. There we find fragments of a prayer related to the Lord's Prayer, signs of the Eucharist, and especially a description of a rite very like Christ's Last Supper. "The procedure for the meeting of the men of reputation when they are called to the banquet held by the party of the Yahad when the Messiah has been revealed among them: the Priest, as head of the entire congregation ... shall enter first, trailed by all his brothers, the Sons of Aaron, those priests appointed to the banquet of the men of reputation. They are to sit before him by rank. Then the Messiah of Israel may enter ... When they gather at the communal table, having set out bread and wine so the communal table is set for eating and the wine (poured) for drinking, none may reach for the first portion of the bread or the wine before the Priest." There is no consensus as to whether the monastery of Qumran is as meaningful to Christians as Bethlehem or Nazareth.

The described community that gathered around the table offering bread and wine is designated by the Hebrew word *yahad*, which is close to the Greek *koinonia*, a concept or attitude we find in Philo of Alexandria and Saul of Tarsus (Paul the Apostle). Certain passages in the Qumran manuscripts herald, perhaps, the Kabbalah: "I took the finest flour mixed with oil together with frankincense as a meal-offering. On all of them I placed salt, and the scent of my burn-offering ascended to heaven." Also found among the scrolls were psalms, where bread was, of course, present. Gilgamesh, too, is mentioned.

To a large degree, holy books became poetic works, as well.

In the Gospels, a reflection of depictions of the world tends to be more prevalent than the depictions themselves. Figures like Herod the Tetrarch of Galilee, whom Flavius Josephus depicted so vividly, or the Roman Procurator Pontius Pilate, who, according to a text discovered in Caesarea, was indeed the *praefectus* of Judea, became symbols in the New Testament, while remaining the personages they were. The historical approach questions and scrutinizes, while the theological reveals and believes. Christ, whose historical existence has been proven, cannot be measured against the idea of Christ in the Christian faith.

It is sometimes just as difficult to bring together as to separate history and theology, bread itself and the Eucharist.

$$\infty\infty$$

After the fall of the Roman Empire, and in spite of Paul's preaching and Peter's work in the Eternal City ("on this rock I shall build my church"), it became increasingly difficult to maintain the religious or ecclesiastical primacy of Rome. Heretic and schismatic strivings manifested themselves in the councils, and were reflected in the clashing views of Church dignitaries, notably bishops. The history of early Christianity is marked by differences that heralded not only a divisive debate but a schism. Pagan customs and Christian rites, the profane and the sacred, doubt and faith, gnosis and credo, confronted and clashed or intersected with each other. For a while, the deep "Antioch schism" came to a stop at the edge of Anatolia. Acacius of Caesarea, who adopted an anti-Nicene position, did not recognize the Holy Spirit as part of the Trinity. Another Acacius, this one from Constantinople, advocated the separation of the Eastern Church from Rome. Photius, also in Constantinople, vehemently defended the anti-Rome position. St. Jerome equated heresy and schism. "Heresy maintains perverse dogma. Schism, by rebellion against the bishop, is a separation from the Church. There is no schism which does not tend to generate for itself some heresy." In his Epistles, St. Cyprian writes about water, salt and wheat flour as ingredients of the Eucharist bread, without ruling out the idea of adding leaven.

For almost 1,000 years after the birth of Christ, Christianity lived with its different views about leavened and unleavened bread. Depending on the circumstances, the one and the other were served at communion. The writings of the first Fathers of the Church reveal no dispute on this subject. But eventually it came and when it did it was to assume an unexpected magnitude.

Before they encountered Graeco-Roman culture, and especially Christianity, Europe's major peoples and their tribes, such as the Germans, Celts and Slavs, as well as smaller ones like the Illyrians, Thracians, Etruscans and others, usually ate roasted or boiled grain. In ancient times, seafarers and Hellenic, Phoenician and who knows what other conquerors brought grains to the islanders of Sicily and Sardinia, Malta and the Baleares. Nomads who had come from Asia, including the Huns, Avars and Turks, neither worked the fields nor sowed grains. Their horsemen took whatever they found along the way, grabbing whatever they could. In embracing Christianity, they adopted not only a faith, but also the bread that went with it.

The Eastern Church and the Western Church undertook, each for itself, to convert the faithful in a way that best suited them. Byzantium and Rome moved away from and confronted each other. In Kiev, towards the end of the tenth century, Russia embraced Christianity under the reign of Prince Vladimir. A magnificent ceremony was held on the banks of the River Don, and it was there that the Grand Prince married Princess Anna Porphyrogenita, sister of the Byzantine emperor Basil II.

The balance of power and influence was leaning towards the East.

The first years of the second millennium of the Christian era had already rolled by when the patriarch of Constantinople Michael I Cerularius announced the schism between the Eastern and Western churches. In the process he condemned those who used unleavened bread in their rites. The bishops in his circle accused Western Christians of falling under the influence of Judaism and Apollinarism. The Patriarchy's treasurer was seen trampling unleavened hosts at the door of a significant city church. For Christian dignitaries in the East, leaven was a sign of the Saviour's human destiny. They called their Catholic brethren *azymites*, prompting the latter to call them *prozymites* or even *fermentarii*, from the Latin for those who ferment. In Rome, the leavened bread made by the Byzantines was disdainfully called *panis cavernosus* ("cavernous bread") – i.e. bread riddled with holes. The word *prozymite* is even to found in the Code of the Serbian tsar Dušan the Mighty.

The schism divided the Balkans. The dualist Bogomil heresy that emerged along the confines dividing the Catholic and Orthodox lands did not concern itself with bread one way or the other, leavened or unleav-ened. Some churches of the East, not only the Armenian but also the Maronite and Malabar, opted for the Western rites and the unleavened host. The Copts did not follow suit. Towards the end of the Middle Ages, the councils of Lyon and Florence tried to settle the dispute. "Our daily bread" of the prayer that is so basic to all Christians could be leavened one day, and unleavened the next. There was no dispute over wine, though, white or red. The biggest spat was over a composite word: *filioque*. In the late sixth century, some Latin Churches added the words "and from the Son" – *filioque* – to the description of the procession of the Holy Spirit (how it relates to other elements of the Holy Trinity of the Father, the Son and the Holy Ghost) in what many Eastern Orthodox Christians have at a later stage argued is a violation of Canon VII of the Council of Ephesus (431 CE)

There were ecclesiastics on either side who tried to avoid or mitigate the break between the churches. In a letter to the Byzantine Patriarch Michael Cerularius, Peter of Antioch noted that the faithful had little concern for the difference between leavened and unleavened bread. After anathemas and excommunications on both sides confirmed the schism, Theophylact of Ohrid, born at Euripus in Euboea, sent a contrite message to his disciple Nicholas, the deacon of St. Sophia: "The Lord ate Pascha at the said hour. Arranged by his disciples and the host who welcomed them, it was prepared according to custom. The Saviour ate the bread before him, unleavened bread. But, thanks to the freedom given to us by Christ, we were not compelled to either take the unleavened or reject the leavened bread. For it is natural for bread to be as available to as many people as possible, even if it be barley bread ... The guests and the host of the Last Supper were accustomed to humble barley bread, the same that, according to the Gospels, was given to the starving crowds." These few lines in my translation were discovered and provided for this occa-sion by the Catholic priests of the Monastic Community of Bose, in the north of Italy, which has a long-standing friendship with Christians of the Eastern rite. For centuries, wheat, barley and rye were cultivated around the Macedonian monastery of St. Naum, where the wise Theophylact left an indelible mark and where he wrote, among other things, the life of St. Clement of Ohrid.

The soil in this region is black, and the rocks white. White bread made of wheat, like black bread made of barley, and even blacker made of rye, are still made and eaten here, as they were in ancient times.

The Armenian Church was one of the first to require that only unleavened bread be used for communion. It remained the only one to do so in the East. Byzantine theologists maintained that the Son of God could have bid farewell to his disciples before Easter, and that ancient Jewish customs did not apply to Christians. Orthodox theology summarized the distinctions it made in three parts: The Gospels say that Jesus held bread (*arton*), not unleavened cakes (*azimos*), in his hand; Catholicism associates Christian liturgy with Jewish custom; leaven in bread is like the soul in the body; leavened bread symbolizes the human fullness of Christ, with all the living force of humanity, in accordance with the Christology of the Council of Chalcedon … As compared to the great celebratory hosts, the small hosts distributed to the faithful divest the rite of its symbolic significance of sharing one single loaf of bread, as described by St. Paul in his Epistle to the Corinthians.

In rejecting the unleavened host, the Orthodox Church chose leavened bread for communion. It also introduced Blessed Bread into its liturgy – first in Greece, in Constantinople and Athens, then in Russia and Ukraine, in Bulgaria and Macedonia, in Serbia and Montenegro, and elsewhere in the Orthodox world. Known as *nafora*, from the Greek *anaphora* (an offering, carrying up), its meaning is connected with the word *antidoron* – "countergift", a gift that announces or replaces communion. These are usually small pieces of bread that the priest distributes by the altar to worshippers, who can take one upon either entering or leaving the church. According to the fifth canon of the *homologetes* Nikephoros, *anaphora* was also the word used for the "consecrated piece". It was given first to impoverished children, and only then to adults. These were the remains of the "showbread" or "presence bread" offered to the church and its priests. Banned by the Council of

Laodicea, the *nafora* returned to the Orthodox Church, especially after the schism, and remained in its liturgy. The Serbian *koljivo*, from the modern Greek word *kolyba*, includes blessing the grain. Wine and sugar are poured over the boiled wheat and it is made for a person's patron saint's day, and in some places for funerals, as well. This recipe, widely adopted, has become a custom, a tradition, a rite.

∞∞∞

Following the schism that divided the Christian world, and the Renaissance that began to open up that world's horizons, clashes broke out among the western churches themselves. The most serious, of course, was caused by Martin Luther, who led the Protestant Christian movement. It shook Europe, especially the central and northern, Germanic and Anglo-Saxon countries. The transformation of the body and blood of Christ into bread and wine was one of, although not the main, reason for the clash. The Reformer saw the Eucharist in terms of the original meaning of the Greek word, as an act of gratitude and mercy, as a gift from God which helps us attain the fullness and joy of faith. For when we pray to God to give us "our daily bread", we are praying, says Luther, "for everything that is necessary in order to have and enjoy daily bread and, on the other hand, against everything which interferes with it." According to the author of *The Large Catechism*, when Christ says of bread "this is my body", he distinguishes that body from all other bodies. Protestantism rejected "transubstantiation", replacing it with "consubstantiation", the doctrine, especially in Lutheran belief, that the substance of the bread and wine coexists with the body and blood of Christ in the Eucharist. Thereafter, the comparison of bread and wine with the body and blood assumes a predominantly symbolic significance. Irritated by Averroes' claim that Christians eat the body and drink the blood of their Lord, Luther retorted: "…it is better for us to eat our God than for the devil to eat us!" Protestants were equally caustic about people who bring pictures of saints or even the pope to church or to processions: "They carry their God in the air, but it is our God who carries us."

Quarrelling with the Church of Rome on the one hand and with Luther and Zwingli on the other, Calvin saw the Eucharistic rite as a "spiritual manducation" (*manducatio*) and was even more vehement in rejecting transubstantiation: "The sacrament does not make Christ become for the first time the bread of life … it calls to remembrance that Christ was made the bread of life that we may constantly eat him, it gives us a taste and relish for that bread and makes us feel its efficacy. For it assures us that whatever Christ did or suffered was done to give us life … and that this quickening is eternal."

When King Henry VIII of England banned religious orders, monastery bakeries still continued to work. The situation did not make bread any the more profane or any the less sacred. Anglicanism leaned towards the kind of reforms advocated by Luther and Calvin, but Catholicism was not about to let itself be ejected from the British Isles, despite the disputes that pitted the king against the pope. Thomas Moore remained a Catholic until his execution, even though he felt that some things needed to be reformed in the Church to which he belonged, particularly, perhaps, certain notions of the Eucharist and transubstantiation. Caught up in the upheavals that shook some of the most celebrated abbeys and priories of the British isles – Beadlow Priory and Turvey Abbey, Arundel Priory and Lyminge Abbey, Folkstone Priory and Dover College, among others – bread shared their fate and was no longer enough to reassure and reunite them.

Instead of embodying Christian unity, the Eucharist became the cause of its rupture. The dispute over transubstantiation and consubstantiation was to last for centuries. Endorsing ideas that stood in opposition to Rome and Catholic dominance, accepting some of Luther's ninety-five theses and Zwingli's sixty-seven articles, along with the teachings of Calvin and the theologians around him, the Reformation rejected, among other things, monastic life and celibacy. Nevertheless, some activities did continue within the walls of the monasteries, such as those connected to libraries (with some modifications of the catalogue), pharmacies and bakeries. For a long time, they made bread just as they had always done. Here and there, this bread even kept the characteristic roughness for which it was known.

The Cistercian monastery of Maulbronn in Baden-Württemberg became a school open to laymen and it was here that Keppler and Hölderlin were educated. The poet complained about the paltry meals and asked his family to send him sugar and coffee. His letters made no mention of bread.

The Austro-Hungarian Empire took a dim view of the infighting between the churches and the monarchy withheld support from the Protestants. In both Bohemia and Slovakia, the Hussite movement brought on a reformist wave that was equally critical of transubstantiation, but the Catholic Church managed to re-establish and re-impose itself. The monasteries preserved their religious culture and traditional way of making bread. In and around the "golden city" of Prague, faith held out a hand to democracy earlier and more than in any other Slavic land. Bread came into play both religiously and socially. The Pannonian Plain, which extends through much of Hungary, is too vast and fertile not to make its own contribution to bread. Few languages have as many words for and sayings about bread as Hungarian.

Squeezed by bigger and/or stronger neighbours – Protestant on the one side and Orthodox on the other – Poland safeguarded Catholicism, sometimes fiercely, as central to its identity. Its famous monasteries, such as Jasna Gora in Częstochowa, home to the famous Black Madonna icon, or the Benedictine Tyniec Abbey on the banks of the Vistula River, or the sites of the great pilgrimage to the monastery church on the hill of St. Anne in Silesia, all celebrate, alongside and within their faith, the traditions of bread. *Pytlowy* and *sitkowy* breads, made with carefully and repeatedly sifted wheat or rye flour, were as purified as anything one could find.

Small nations were hard put to cope with the conflicts imposed on them by bigger and more powerful states and religions, along with the Eastern and Western Church. The Balkan mosaic, where numerous tribes lived in lands sandwiched between the Byzantine and Roman spheres of influence, offers many a tragic example. Almost everything that can be said has already been said about relations between Catholics and the Orthodox, Croats, Serbs, Montenegrins, Slovenes, Macedonians in this region. But it is worth stopping to mention the experience of the Albanians. Their ancestors – Illyrians and also possibly Thracians –

first adopted Christianity, and then largely converted to Islam. But they were less divided by their religion than their neighbours, being first and foremost Albanians, *Shqiptar* in their language, and only then followers of Islam or the Western or Eastern Church. Bread in their language is called *bukë* or *bukë e zezë* if it is black bread. Generations of the poor and hungry swore by bread as if it were a god: *pasha bukën*, "so help me bread". No one else in the Balkans or beyond talks of their bread in this way. And no one knows where the word comes from, whether it is derived from Illyrian or Thracian, or perhaps Latin or Venetian. Some think it is rooted in the word *bocca* (mouth, morsel). *Bucca panis*, the celebrated *arbiter elegantiae* Petronius once wrote.

Voltaire wrote ironically about the "extravagant blasphemy whereby people say that three gods make one", or "the idea of eating the God they adore", only to digest and transform it into excrement. In *Resurrection*, Tolstoy describes how an Orthodox priest, "dressed in a strange and very inconvenient garb, made of gold cloth, cut and arranged little bits of bread on a saucer, and then put them into a cup with wine, repeating at the same time different names and prayers", turning the bread and wine into "the flesh and blood of God ... Fulfilling the demands of this faith, he had for years been able to draw an income, which enabled him to keep his family."

Lev Nikolayevich Tolstoy, who said he believed in Jesus Christ, was excommunicated by the Russian Church.

∇∇∇

Power and influence in society and in the Church, social status and hierarchy were even reflected in the names and types of bread. The feudal order was loath to give up its privileges. French terminology illustrates this only too well: *pain de cour* – at the court of the king; *pain de pape* – in the curiae and bishoprics; *pain de sacristie* or *de chapitre* – for the priests and the religious; *pain de chevalier* – in the houses of the nobility; *pain d'écuyer* – for squires; and finally, the cheaper and more modest *pain de boulanger* – in the ordinary bakery. The secularization and laicization that came with the

Enlightenment, propagated in different European countries under different names – the Siècle des Lumières, Aufklärung and others – encouraged new ways of seeing the world and religion. And with that came different notions of bread, the need for and the right to bread. In his *Encyclopaedia*, the philosopher Denis Diderot says that "religion is not about decorating temples to please our eyes or ears … Let us love our neighbours like ourselves, and consequently be always attentive to do them good, or at least always careful not to do them evil … This is precisely the religion prescribed to us by God…" Too much, he says, is spent on "decorating altars, for example, and on the pomp of ceremonies … This is crass and deceptive piety, with little in common with the spirit of Christianity, which is inspired only by beneficence and fraternal charity." Diderot writes these words in the very chapter on consecrated bread.

Some philosophers of the Enlightenment believed that bread could improve religion by virtue of the modesty it embodies. Others rejected any discussion of the subject. Bread progressed from being a prayer to becoming a demand. It left the realm of religion and entered the sphere of justice. This path – from prayer to demand and from religion to justice – was a thorny one, as well.

It is not easy to escape the way of the cross.

The year 1788, on the eve of the French Revolution, witnessed a terrible harvest and was marked by drought and hunger. Millers were accused of adding sand and sawdust to the grain, bakers of mixing chaff and bran with the flour, and both of adulterating and masking wheat to make more money and of "speculating" with the price of bread. The people of France rose up and rebelled. In the streets and squares they demanded *pain d'égalité* – the "bread of equality". The rebels stormed the Bastille. The king, who had proven incapable of coming to their aid, was guillotined, and with him the queen who, surprised to learn that the people had no bread, said, according to an anecdote: "Let them eat cake."

"Bread, bread!" That may have been the only rallying cry or slogan that never betrayed the people who shouted it and who stood up for it, in the hope of vanquishing poverty and attaining justice. The rest is history, sometimes kind, sometimes tolerable, but most often painful and brutal.

IV.
SEVEN
CRUSTS

The paths forged by grain and bread often left traces that the past was unable to bequeath to history, and history failed to transmit to the future. Some are so scattered that they are barely recognizable and hard to decipher.

The number *seven*, as in "seven lean-fleshed kine" (cows) often appears when evoking years of famine or similar events, although it does not exclusively refer to disastrous times. In *Book of Revelation*, St. John mentions "seven stars", "seven seals", "seven trumpets" and "seven dishes of God's anger". According to Persian tradition, seven different kinds of food are served for *Nowruz*, the New Year, their names all beginning with the letter *S* – a custom known as *haft Sin*. In the Quran, the Prophet Muhammad speaks of "seven paths", "seven seas", "seven heavens", "seven nights" and "seven green ears of grain".

"Seven crusts of bread" is an expression used in many dialects in the Mediterranean and elsewhere, although no one knows when it was first used. Legend has it that it was coined by sailors at sea for long periods of time, who almost broke their teeth trying to eat the hard, stale bread.

Human destiny, be it collective or individual, depended on bread in various ways and to varying degrees. Lack of it, even when by choice, was the cause of great suffering, especially among ascetics, hermits and monks, pilgrims, sailors and prisoners, the poor, beggars and, among others, the Roma. And yet, despite everything, "seven-crusted bread" nourished both their bodies and their souls.

I have given this book seven chapters.

∽∽∽

The lives and sufferings of three saints named John are associated with bread: St. John the Evangelist, St. John Chrysostom and St. John the Baptist.

The first, son of Zebedee and brother of St. James the Elder, was the youngest of Christ's twelve apostles, and the disciple Jesus loved the most, as did he indeed love Jesus. At the Last Supper, he leaned "on Christ's breast" and after the latter's death became a second son to the Mother of God. He then travelled around Judea with Peter, preaching the new faith; walked on foot across the desert, eating bread and grasshoppers; and established seven churches in Anatolia. At one point he was persecuted and thrown into a cauldron of boiling oil, only to be saved by divine intervention and left miraculously unscathed. St. John the Evangelist is believed to have written the *Book of Revelation* during his exile on the island of Patmos, following the example of the prophets Ezekiel and Daniel of the Old Testament.

The second St. John was born in Antioch, in what is today southern Turkey, a city surrounded by fields of grain. He was called Chrysostom ("the golden-mouthed") because of the eloquence of his preaching. He was successively a monk, a patriarch, a hermit and a prisoner, and more importantly one of the four great Church Fathers of Eastern Christianity. Bread and wine, and their transformation into the body and blood of Christ, occupy a special place in his homilies, so often dedicated to the Eucharist. And it should be remembered that dry loaves of bread were his main, sometimes his only source of nourishment during his years of retreat and exile.

St. John the Baptist preceded Christ and is known as "the Fore-runner" (*Prodromos*). He was probably close to the Essenes of the Dead Sea and was familiar with their teachings. His mother Elizabeth was a relative of the Virgin Mary's, and he famously baptized Jesus in the River Jordan. He also condemned Herod the Tetrach for his sacrilegious marriage with Herodias, causing Herod's fury and Salome's apparent wish to have him killed. He was tortured and then beheaded. John the Baptist preached *metanoia*, a kind of rebirth of the soul. He spent a long time roaming the desert, with only a coarse hair shirt for clothing, and "wild honey and grasshoppers" for food. However, although the passage in the Gospel According to St. Matthew about the saint's life of absti-nence may not mention grasshoppers (*akridos* in Greek), it could have been referring to carob, a linguistic confusion that might have happened when translating from the Aramaic, the language in which St. Matthew was writing. In some places, especially the islands, carob bread is called "St. John's bread". St. John the Baptist and his beheading are depicted in innumerable works of art: he appears in a mosaic in Ravenna, and on the portals of the cathedrals of Chartres and Amiens. Leonardo da Vinci once painted him as a child next to the Virgin Mary, and another time as an enigmatic young man. Poets tried to describe the dance of the cruel Salome and the tragic end of the saint, who died starving, without even a crust of bread.

Among the most venerated saints are two Anthonys. The first, known as Anthony the Abbot, Anthony of the Desert and Anthony the Great, was born in 251 ce in Egypt, in a town called Coma (modern-day Queman), near Beni-Suef, not far from the Red Sea. The other, born in Lisbon, is known as St. Anthony of Padua because he left a deep mark on the city and it was there that he died. St. Athanasius wrote about him, describing a life full of miracles.

St. Anthony the Great lived in Fayyum and Pispir, a mountain by the Nile, preaching the Christian faith. Following Christ's example, he retreated into the desert. After overcoming the temptations Satan laid before him, he founded the order of anchorites. Painters and printmakers such as Hieronymus Bosch and Jacques Callot depicted his visions and many writers, Gustave Flaubert included, have described them. His spirit defended itself against his body, and his body defended itself against itself. Bread and water gave him sustenance.

The martyr Anthony came from ancient Egypt to visit Paul the Hermit, known as the Anchorite of Thebes. Legend has it that a raven brought them bread every day – first to Paul, and then to both of them. There are many paintings of the black bird carrying a piece of bread in its beak. It would feed other hermits, as well, among them St. Jerome who, alone in his cave, was filling reams of pages with his translations. St. Anthony the Great lived for 105 years, performing miracles, healing those sick with the plague, leprosy and especially epilepsy, which was caused by ergot from the barley in the bread eaten by the poor. At the age of 105, he went to the Red Sea and Mount Quizum, where the monastery bearing his name has been partially preserved. During the days leading up to his death, he lived off only bread and water.

At Mount Quizum this bread is still revered and considered sacred.

St. Anthony of Padua was born almost 1,000 years later. He did not live nearly so long as his great namesake. He was thirty-six years old when he drew his last breath and the sisters of the Poor Clare monastery at Arcella, near Padua, closed his eyes forever. He, too, had vowed to live the life of a hermit, retreating into the severe, inaccessible hermitage of Monte Paolo in the region of Emilia Romagna. The miracles he performed have inspired books and paintings, and it was said that he could talk to birds. A piece of bread and a jug of water were the sole items on his table. The only time he drank wine was for the Easter celebrations.

One day a passer-by challenged St. Anthony of Padua, wagering that when hungry, his mule would prefer a few oats to the Host. They gave it nothing to eat for two days; on the third day the mule refused the oats and knelt down before the consecrated bread, and thus the disbeliever was converted to the faith of Christ. The Church then gave the name of the two saints to the alms distributed to the hungry, thus uniting Anthony the Great, the Hermit and Anthony of Padua, the Miracle

Worker. "St. Anthony's bread" is food for the poor, the helpless and the wretched. It has saved not only the religious from hunger, but the irreligious, as well.

St. Francis was born in Assisi, a village dating from the days of the Roman Empire. It was also the birthplace of the poet Propertius. A temple and a sculpture of Minerva used to stand in its central square, and ramparts encircled the city to protect the populace. Young Francis gave the builders a helping hand and in the process acquired knowledge that proved useful when he decided to build the Chapel of San Damiano. His father was a prosperous merchant and his mother was originally from Provence. Their table offered a choice of the finest breads made in Umbria and the south of France at the time. During the war between Assisi and Perugia, young Francis was captured and spent a year in prison, living only on bread and water. Both his jailers and his fellow inmates were surprised to see how bravely he endured his punishment. When he finally left his cell, he decided to give up his life of ease for the life of "the Holy Gospel". He broke off relations with his father, sold his share of the family property and gave all the proceeds to the poor. Considered strange, and even ignorant, he took no interest in the contemporary dispute between the "nominalists" and the "realists" concerning the status of universals – roundness, goodness, etc. – which the realists asserted existed independently as Platonic ideals, while the nominalists argued to the contrary. When he arrived in Rome and asked the pope to approve the "regula" that he had composed for his brotherhood, some of the Holy Father's advisors mocked him, calling him *simplex et idiota*.

His first attempt at a pilgrimage to the Holy Land was thwarted by strong winds. The ship on which he was travelling had to turn back and change course for the islands of the Adriatic. His second attempt, during the Crusades, took him to Egypt and gave him the opportunity to meet sultan al-Malik al Kamil in Damietta. With a white rope belting his dark tunic, a beard on his face and his head tonsured, he made his way through the rows of surprised soldiers to the Turkish sultan. Hagiography depicts this meeting as an attempt by Francis to establish a dialogue between their religions and peoples. The Islamic side left no written record of this meeting. Voltaire saw the sultan as a tolerant successor of Saladin who was being confronted by a Christian fanatic. The future saint was appalled by the massacres and lootings he witnessed, perpetrated under the pretext of "liberating Jerusalem". He ate bread, which he shared with his fellow voyagers after blessing it.

The work and example of St. Francis resonated far and wide. Among the first to accept it were the monks in French abbeys, notably the Benedictines at Vézelay and the Cistercians, both occupied with daily working the land and adept at making bread. In addition to hagiographies celebrating Francis, there are also the *fioretti* relating episodes from his life, which very often mention bread. Once, by the Lake of Perugia, he was "inspired by God to observe Lent that year on one of the islands of the lake". Francis spent all forty days of Lent eating nothing but half a loaf of bread, "setting aside any temptation to vainglory". He was especially fond of the "bread of charity", "consecrated with love and gratitude". He and the brethren of his order would beg in the towns and villages, sometimes going barefoot. One of the preserved *fioretti* relates his sermon to the birds, inviting them to "praise God". After seeing the birds "soar up into the air in one flock with wondrous songs" he encountered a man whose sack contained only a little bit of bread. The two of them started to distribute it to the poor on the outskirts of the city, yet the sack remained full. A similar miracle happened at a cloister of the Poor Clares. Clare, the future saint and founder of the order that bears her name, a friend and possible beloved of St. Francis in his youth, asked him to cut the one remaining small loaf of bread into fifty slices, one for each of the nuns. It seemed an impossible task yet everyone received as much bread as they wanted. Thus the experience of the prophet Elisha, who fed the many with just a little bread, was repeated.

After he was transported from Mount La Verna to the small town of La Porziuncola, near Assisi, the dying St. Francis asked his brethren to prepare a "last supper". His contemporary Thomas de Celano witnessed these moments. "The brothers wept torrents of tears at this spectacle, and, sighing heavily, they succumbed to their excessively great pain and compassion." Francis asked them to bring him bread; he then blessed it, broke it into pieces and shared them with everyone. Then he said he wished to hear an extract from the Gospel According to St. John, which starts with the words: "And the Jews' Passover was at hand" and Christ's message from the Gospel: "I am the bread of life; he that cometh to me shall never hunger." As the next morning dawned – in the autumn of 1226 – a flock of larks flew over the hut where the saint took communion, then passed away.

∽∽∽

Monks whose vows and faith inspired their life, which they completely sacrificed to God, are, in their way, saints and martyrs themselves. Their chosen path is one of endurance and prayer. Some, even before Christ, were hermits, as early Christian monasticism drew inspiration from the examples of the Prophet Elijah and John the Baptist, who both lived alone in the desert. Fasting brought them closer to salvation; bread helped them survive. According to St. Chrysostom, "fasting is followed by its sister and companion, prayer ... Fasting, which finds us slaves and prisoners, loosens the bonds and delivers us from the tyranny, and restores us to our former freedom." Ephraim the Syrian bequeathed to posterity an inspired message: fasting, he said, "is the path of repentance and the inducement of tears ... Fasting brings peace to our homes ... Fasting is a chariot to heaven ... Fasting does not admit the remembrance of wrongs ... It brings wisdom to lawgivers."

Others who fasted, each in their own way, were the reclusive anchorites, disciples of St. Anthony, and the communal coenobites, disciples of St. Pachomius. In Upper Egypt, the desert of Thebaid welcomed them. Like Abraham, the hermit left behind his home, his family and his traditions. The hermits followed the example of the pre-Christian and Christian prophets, and above all Christ himself when he spent forty days in the desert, and adopted a strict and demanding rule of life. Despite their practice of mortification and suffering, they preserved a sense of reason and volition.

Hermits listened to the silence and responded with a silence of their own. They were guided by the Holy Scriptures. "They spoke to the Holy Scriptures and the Scriptures spoke to them." Prayer and meditation filled their lives. Their sayings, those that were not scattered by the wind or buried in the sand, are called *apophthegmata* and are preserved in various collections known as the *Apophthegmata Patrum*, where bread is a constant presence. We learn from them that the hermit would offer a visitor "dry bread and salt", along with vinegar.

In those parts of Egypt where Coptic monuments have been preserved, bread differs little from the way it was made in the days of the pharaohs. One can recognize its shape in the faded frescoes of the monastery of St. Macarius, surrounded by the solitude of sand and the silhouettes of the rocks. If you pass by St. Bishoi you will see the monks who still live in the ancient building, still making bread the way they once used to. The kneaded dough is first laid out in the sun until it acquires a soft, smooth, thin crust; then salt is added and the dough is placed in the oven until it is completely done, all the while retaining something of the sun that warmed it. The monks in the Scetes Desert of Wadi al Natrun, known as "Syrians", make bread the same way. The Baramus monastery, located in the same region, has a huge wall painting that depicts Melchizedek offering bread and wine to Abraham. Young monks carry bread at the Qusur el-Rubaiyat monastery in the *kellia* ("the cells"), a fourth-century Egyptian Christian monastic community spread out over many square miles in the Nitrian Desert – referred to as "the innermost desert". Heliopolis once stood where the districts of Musturud and el Matareya are now. Legend has it that the members of the Holy Family passed through here as they fled the massacre ordered by Herod. Long ago, pilgrims would make their way there; some still do even today. Under a scrawny sycamore tree, a monk with a long grey beard offers a traveller bread that looks like a huge host. The Copts, at great cost to themselves, preserved their Christian customs and remain true to them. Bread helped them to safeguard their own identity.

In the second half of the twentieth century in Ethiopia, with its ancient churches that lean against the red rocks, I found a few monks still remaining. One of them was Ezana. He took his name from the king of Axum, who adopted Christianity in the fourth century. Ezana explained to me softly: "Our brothers walked these narrow corridors, cleft out of the rocks. They sang old hymns, prayed, took communion. The Ethiopian Church found itself straddling the East and the West, independent of both. It preserved its autonomy. Pilgrims built black Jerusalem on this plain. Bread is revered here, even though there is never enough of it. Oil, too, is revered, rare though it is. There is practically no wine in this region."

On the western side of the Mediterranean, the Rule of St. Benedict prescribed the average measure of bread the monastery needed on working and non-working days. St. Benedict was familiar with the experience of his great predecessors, especially the *Rules of Pachomius*, which had been translated by St. Jerome, the patron saint of translators: *Panis libra una propensa sufficit* ("a generous pound of bread is enough for a day, whether for only one meal or for both dinner and supper ... Should it happen that the work is heavier than usual, the abbot may decide – and he will have the authority – to grant something additional, provided that it is appropriate, and that above all overindulgence is avoided, lest a monk experience indigestion. For nothing is so inconsistent with the life of any Christian as overindulgence. Our Lord says: 'Take care that your hearts are not weighed down with overindulgence' (Luke 21:34)." These were the rules St. Benedict prescribed, and the Benedictines were always industrious; through their work they maintained a balance between body and spirit, inviting the faithful to respect bread and revere communion.

Some monasteries strained to ensure that there was enough food. Bread was made for the whole week and sometimes for a whole month in advance. Monks wishing to pay penance let the bread turn hard, or, in order not to overindulge, ate it in small morsels. The bread varied from one monastery to the next. In the Greek monastic region of Meteora, for example, the bread was different from that in Spanish, Italian, Croatian or Slovenian monasteries. In Greek and Russian monasteries, traditions regarding bread outlived the monasteries themselves. The same is true of Ukrainian, Bulgarian, Serbian, Macedonian and Montenegrin monasteries.

In one of the three "horns" of the Halkidiki peninsula stands Mount Athos, the Holy Mountain. Here bread is especially revered. Indeed, according to one of the patriarchs, "an eternal seed" was sown here. Dion, Thyssos, Kleones, Olophyxos, Acrothoi are the names of some of the towns and villages that predate the first monastery. The people who lived there were familiar with many kinds of bread, some of which are mentioned by Chrysippus of Tyana in his *Artopoikon*. From time immemorial, ascetics, hermits and coenobites converged here: they lived in caves, ate wild herbs and plants, drank rainwater. It was centuries before monastic life began in the Athos peninsula, and the Great Lavra monastery (*Mehistis Lavras*) was built. Built by the rulers of Eastern Orthodox countries, twenty monasteries are housed on the Holy Mountain, called *Agion oros* by the Greeks. It was agreed that this number sufficed and should not be exceeded. Several centuries before the birth of Christ, the ships of Persian general Mardonius sank in front of Mount Athos; and Hellada was saved by a storm. Nearby is the town of Stagira, Aristotle's birthplace, although never enamoured of its illustrious son, and the city of Salonika, where the Sephardim found refuge. They were adept at making unleavened bread, in keeping with Jewish law.

Mount Athos is covered with underbrush in some places, and starkly bare in others. In the spring, when the broom blossoms, it turns a resplendent yellow. Sometimes, in the distance, you can see Mount Olympus with the naked eye. All around are quarries, exploited and depleted by the construction of the monasteries and churches. Bordering the narrow winding paths, cypress, chestnut, oak and elm trees grow, and there, too, are both wild and cultivated olive trees. The passer-by may wonder which of these trees offers the best wood to fuel the bread ovens built next to the monasteries.

Along the shores of Mount Athos, there are few welcoming piers; in the autumn and winter it is a windy place, especially on the north-eastern side. Seagulls fly over the promontories in flocks, as if they, like the monks, prefer to stay together. The surrounding sea waters are clean and translucent, with jagged rocks, sharpened by the breaking waves, jutting out from the shallows. Streams wend their way down from the hinterland and into the sea; in the summer, most of them run dry.

Mount Athos is also a place where no women are allowed.

The St. Panteleimon monastery stands within reach of the sea. Its green cupolas and gilded crosses glisten in the light of the sun and the moon. It was once home to more than 2,000 Russian monks; today there are fewer than 100. Guardians of the vestiges of the past, they pray together – and in solitude. A narrow path leads to their bakery, where there is a huge oven, covered in white stone on the outside and lined with brick on the inside. Its iron door is more than 6 ft (2 m) wide and perhaps 33 ft (10 m) high. Similar bread ovens can be found in other Greek monasteries on Mount Athos and in the Serbian monastery of Hilandar. The ovens are fuelled with wood, usually from oak trees, and sometimes from wild olive trees. The logs are left to dry in the sun for a long time, to ensure that they provide more ember than flame. Twigs of broom are sometimes tossed onto the fire to give the bread their fragrance, in what may be a leftover from an ancient, forgotten rite.

Three kinds of bread are usually made in these sacred places: white wheat bread, with a soft crust, so that even the elderly, sometimes toothless, priors can eat it with their gums; black rye bread, which is quite hard and intended for the younger monks; and "long-lasting bread", made with different kinds of flour, for anchorites who do not live in the monastery. The *nafora* (fried and seasoned stale bread) awaits the faithful in the narthex of the church or at its door. The daily bread served to the monks is kept for seven days, sometimes longer, as long as it is edible. The Russians, in keeping with their tradition, use what is left to brew a "bread beer" known as *kvass*, which is good for quenching one's thirst. And they use the mould, as well: the old priests know that it contains curative properties and that in olden times it was used to dress wounds. The water used to make the dough is not taken from just any well, as some streams are said to be "healthier" than others. The wind is also taken into account: "if the air is too disturbed, the colour of the bread will be lighter," one prior tells us. When it is too humid, the dough relaxes and falls flat. Here they make only leavened bread, and there is no occasion when they eat unleavened bread. Everyone on Mount Athos abides by this rule – the Serbs, the Macedonians, the Romanians, the Georgians, the Bulgarians, the Ukrainians and, especially, the Russians.

Their faith brings them closer, bread unites them.

The Greek monasteries of Mount Athos have more varieties of bread than anywhere else. The monastery of Karakala, on the north-eastern side of Halkidiki, as well as those of Filothei, Zograf and Pantokratoros, may retain the closest connection to the ancient Hellenic traditions. Coptic monks from the deserts of Ethiopia, from Sinai, from Armenian sanctuaries at the foot of Ararat once came here. They knew the oldest Christian customs and brought them along. In the *kellia*, no one ate freshly made bread, it was prepared for the following day. Archpriest Porphyrios of Mt. Athos (1906–91), who was made a saint in 2013, was inspired by St. Zenon the Faster, who asked to be immured in one of caves at the Kyiv Pechersk Lavra (Kiev Monastery of the Caves) in a narrow cell with a slit just big enough to push through a bit of bread and water. There are still monks on Mount Athos living isolated on the surrounding cliffs, their only shelter a hut made of twigs and branches, with stone slabs called "deserts" for a floor. "They are following the example of Christ and St. John in the desert," a deacon told me during one of my seasonal visits to this place. In the winter, the wind and cold and sometimes snow make it difficult to reach them. Once a month, a young, strong "brother" is dispatched to the ascetics and hesychasts, with a basket of hard, long-lasting bread. When moistened, the loaf softens but still retains its pungency. A traveller once noted that "The bread of the Holy Mountain tastes like *humus*."

The names of the Athonite priests are recorded in the pages of the annals: Athanasius the Athonite, builder of the Great Lavra; Joseph the Hesychast, advocate of "inner peace"; Nicodemus the Hagiorite, called a saint before he was ever canonized. Ephraim of Katounakia and Vartolomei and Tikhon, both from Kapsala, are also mentioned. Inscribed on their tombs are the words: "One does not live by bread alone, but also by prayer."

Among the *apophthegmata* of father Paissos, preserved in the archives of the Holy Mountain, is one that says: "After fasting bread tastes sweet."

Across the Mediterranean Sea from Greece, at the foot of Mount Sinai, in the middle of the desert that stretches all the way to the Red Sea, is St. Catherine's Monastery, named after the martyr tortured under the rule of Diocletian. Within its walls, next to the Chapel of the Burning Bush, is a small Fatimid mosque frequented by the Bedouins of Djebel. Only a few monks remain from what was once a much larger community. Solitude resonates at every step. Preserved in the monastery's treasury is the *Codex Sinaiticus*, with a copy of the Greek translation of the Old Testament, known as the *Septuaginta*. It is a miracle that the various invaders who stormed through here spared the monastery. It has been the beneficiary of gifts from European kings, Turkish sultans, Russian tsars – even Ivan the Terrible himself. To this day, the Bedouins help the monks to make both leavened and unleavened bread, following the steps that have been practised since biblical times. No one who has tasted the bread of Sinai will ever forget it. It has no equal, not in Jerusalem and not in Istanbul.

Impressed on it is the seal of St. Catherine the Martyr.

Pilgrimages are as old as religion itself, sometimes even older. The first pilgrims belonged to peoples who have since died out along with their rites and rituals. For centuries pilgrims travelled to holy sites by land and by sea, crossing deserts and fording rivers. And always, their main food staple was bread.

In ancient times, Egyptians would go on pilgrimage to Thebes, Luxor, Karnak, Abydos. In Hebron, the Hebrews searched for the tombs of their patriarchs, went to see the ruins of the Temple in Jerusalem and visited Gilgal, Bersabe, Bethel. For as long as it was possible for them to do so, they visited the tombs of Nahum and Ezra, in modern-day Iraq, or of Esther in Iran. Until the destruction of the Temple, pilgrims coming from Sinai, Judea or Samaria made a major pilgrimage to Jerusalem three times a year. One of the Three Pilgrimage Festivals is known as *sukkot*: a special bread was made for the pilgrims before they set out.

The ancient Greeks consulted the Oracle of Delphi, gathered at Eleusis to celebrate the Eleusinian Mysteries and visited places dedicated to Zeus, Poseidon or Demeter, Dionysus, Hermes, Aphrodite and other gods. The three biggest pilgrimages in the history of Christianity were to Jerusalem, Rome and Santiago de Compostela. Today as in the past, Muslims from all over the world go on pilgrimage to Mecca and Medina.

In the Middle Ages, Christian pilgrims, especially Catholics, embarked on a long, arduous journey – called *itinera peregrinationis*. They prepared themselves spiritually and received the blessing of the Church before setting out, and on the eve of their departure they sought and offered forgiveness. They took little with them: a tunic with arm slits (known as a *pèlerine* in French, from the word *pèlerin*, meaning pilgrim), a broad-brimmed hat, sandals, a walking stick to lean on (*bourdon* in French, *bordone* in Italian). Hanging from their shoulder was a satchel, containing, among other things, a slice of bread and a dry gourd filled with water – just enough to cover the distance between one stop on the journey and the next. Some held in their hand a burning candle, or a heavy object, often a stone, as an instrument to practise mortification. The latter needed more bread than the others to sustain them.

What distinguished the pilgrims was their demeanour and comport-ment. Inspired by their faith and self-sacrifice, sustained by charity and compassion, threatened with fatigue and illness, they found refuge in churches and monasteries. St. Ephraim the Syrian founded the first hos-pital for pilgrims on the road to Jerusalem in the fourth century CE. The Order of St. John of Jerusalem, better known as the Order of Malta, as well as the Templars, the Cistercians, Benedictines, Franciscans and others offered help and protection. The better-off pilgrims purchased papal indul-gences, which served as passes and made it easier for them to get bread.

On the roads leading to Santiago de Compostela in the northwest of Spain, the faithful used the *Codex calixtinus*, whose Book V was called "The Pilgrim's Guide". Thanks to its advice and warnings, the pilgrims knew what awaited them at the next stopping point, where they would be able to get bread, find an overnight dwelling place, perhaps even a bed. They would stop at the monastery of St. Isidore in Léon, where they drew fresh, regenerating water from the Bernesga River. There they would receive communion and replenish their provisions. One of the last stopping points was the little town of Arzúa, surrounded by "flowering meadows and limpid springs", where the best bread in Galicia was to be found, near the great gate to the city. The pilgrims received their warmest welcome at the Chapel of Madalena and Church of St. Mary Magdalene, maintained by the Augustinians. In the seventeenth century, Pope Paul V abolished the blessing of the walking stick and the satchel, but the bread continued to be blessed and so remained forever: *panis peregrinus*, the bread of the pilgrim, fortified and comforted the exhausted pilgrims as they approached Santiago de Compostela.

Travelling to Jerusalem on Venetian vessels was just as difficult and more expensive. For food the pilgrims had a paltry ration of ship's biscuit, with a few meagre mouthfuls of gruel, and the galleys were often intercepted by pirates who robbed both crew and passengers. Using the land route via the Balkans could prove more hazardous still. The local bands of *Hajduks* were as bad as the pirates, and the *Uskoks* rivalled both. As the Ottoman Empire advanced almost to Palestine during the 1500s, the risks increased and fewer and fewer pilgrimages were made.

There was still bread to be found in the caravanserais, but the atmosphere there was unpropitious for "infidels".

And so the journey to Rome, all the difficulties notwithstanding, was the easier and more bearable. At almost every monastery, in almost every refectory, the pilgrims could get a piece of bread, a bowl of soup and a glass of wine. A little-known guide from the end of the Middle Ages, translated from the Latin, gives the pilgrim the following advice: "It is good to set out around the middle of August (*circa medium augustum*), when the air is warm and the road dry ... while the granaries are still full with the new harvest"; in other words, when there is more bread and it is easier to obtain. This is why the pilgrims' road to Rome, notably the *Via francigena*, became so celebrated. In paintings, sculptures and literature the memory of the central spiritual and corporal importance of bread lived on, and became our own.

The Quran enjoins Muslims whose incomes so permit to make a pilgrimage, known as the *Hadj*, to Mecca and Medina in the last month of the Islamic calendar and to gather in front of the *Kaaba*. There they can then receive the blessings of *baraka*, whereby their sins are forgiven. Once the pilgrimage is completed, they are awarded the title *Hadji*. If poor health or old age prevents someone from going on the pilgrimage by themselves, they have the right to choose and reward someone to do so in their name. The *Hadj* is not without its own travails, for crossing the desert has its perils. Some Bedouins did not hesitate to attack and rob the caravans, watching for and choosing the most opportune moment to do so. It was important to make sure that everything was secured and protected, especially at night. The bread made en route on the embers of camel dung was not to everyone's taste, so before setting off, the Muslim pilgrim would make sure to provide himself with good bread and to put on the special white garment worn for the occasion, called an *ihram*.

The long road that links the Persian Gulf with the Red Sea passes through Jedda, the famous departure point for the pilgrimage – the first stage on the road to Medina, Mecca and finally the *Kaaba*, the imposing cuboid structure made of black stone known as the "hand of God" (*jamin Allah*). Djibril (Gabriel) brought it to Ibrahim (Abraham) so that work could begin on building the future sanctuary. The pilgrim must circle it seven times, moving in a counterclockwise direction. This is the ritual of *tawaf*. Young pilgrims must also walk back and forth between the hills of al-Safa and al-Marwa seven times. This is the ritual of *sa'y*. Once they have completed their journey to the holy sites, the pilgrims change back into the clothes they were wearing before prayers and then head for Mount Arafat. For this occasion they are advised not to eat anything heavy but rather to limit themselves to a few bites of light bread, a slice of raghifa or *rakika*.

Arab chroniclers created a special literary genre, the *rihla*, which refers to both the journey and the written account of that journey, including descriptions of sanctuaries, the *Hadj* and the bread. Ibn Jubayr, born in Valencia, Spain, observed and described the lively crowds thronging around the sanctuaries. The twelfth- and thirteenth-century Persian traveller, Al Harawi, was enchanted by the beauty of the rites and rituals.

Ibn Battuta, one of the most talented travel writers, immortalized religious and secular scenes around the Grand Mosque in Damascus. From the east and north it was easier to approach the Kaaba by travelling through Anatolia and avoiding the desert. Turkish bread – *ekmek* – and the thin *yufka*, which becomes soft with just a few drops of water – sustained the pilgrims on their journey.

An imam in Damascus advised us to look for bread in places that bear the stamp of the past and of the history of Islam, such as the site where the sword of Dawud lies, or the staff of Musa, the hair from Muhammad's beard, the remains of Yahya's (John the Baptist's) hand, the original manuscript of the Quran, the swords of the first four caliphs, the gilded box containing the Black Stone (*Hajar al-Aswad*), the keys to door of the Kaaba. It is in these places and next to these objects, they say, that real bread is to be found.

But to get to them, one must often first eat "seven-crusted bread".

◊◊◊

Along the coasts of the Baltic and the Atlantic, as well as inland, towns sprouted up where bread was younger than in the Mediterranean, but just as tasty. The following list was taken from a calendar printed in Amsterdam around 100 years ago: Hamburg, Stockholm, Copenhagen, Oslo, Helsinki, Vilnius – once known as the Jerusalem of the North, Bordeaux, and then farther in from the coast, Paris, Lyon, Berlin and Brussels, in Central Europe Vienna, Munich, Frankfurt, Geneva, Krakow and Warsaw, "golden Prague", Zagreb and Ljubljana, and moving eastwards, Budapest, Bucharest, Belgrade, Sofia, Skopje and Tirana. The list is certainly incomplete but it is long enough even as it is. All these cities witnessed times of want and times of plenty, and with them different kinds of bread, white and dark, good and bad, some even with "seven crusts".

The desert in the south and the cold in the north mark the boundaries of the wheat fields. The peoples of Europe, Asia, Africa, both Americas and elsewhere passed on to each other their experience and their skills in agriculture. The migration of grains increased the population, especially on the old continent. Before clashing with the Romans and encountering Christianity, the Germans knew little about bread. Caesar observed that they had "no interest in agriculture" (*agriculturae non studentes*). In the early Middle Ages they worshipped their own goddess of fertility, Freya, the "mother of cereals", but only gradually did they became excellent bakers. They penetrated Russia from the north, notably from Prussia, where the land was not particularly fertile and the bread was usually dark. They were welcomed in the plains of Russia and Ukraine, which were vast but poorly cultivated in those troubled times.

Followers of the "old faith" in Russia, heirs of the *raskolniki*, who were loyal to the old rituals, revered bread and considered it a pledge of faith. In Russia's past, there were "seekers of God" – *bogoiskatelyi* – for whom bread was more than food; rather it was something sacred. Close to their worldview were the "barefooted" (*bosiaki*), who sought redemption, lived an ascetic life away from any monastic community, existing simply on just bread and water.

Wishing, as the poet Pushkin put it, to open "a window onto Europe", Peter the Great of Russia adopted from his neighbours what he considered their best. Catherine the Great was German by origin. The meeting of the two peoples could have been happier than it was, had history but allowed it. German bakers to the west and Greek monks to the east were worthy teachers. On the eve of two revolutions, the best bread in Europe was made in St. Petersburg, on the Neva River. That, at least, was what White Russian émigrés liked to say.

In exile they ate their black bread with seven (and who knows how many more) crusts.

And so one century followed another, bringing new pilgrimages and reaffirming some of the old ones. Among them are the famous pilgrim sites of Lourdes, Fatima, Chartres, Assisi and Mount Athos. There are lesser-known sanctuaries also worth mentioning: Jasna Gora in Częstochowa, Poland; Marija Bistrica and Trsat in Croatia, dedicated to the Virgin Mary; the basilica of San Nicola in Bari; and others, some far away from the Mediterranean coast, like the earlier mentioned Kyiv Pechersk Lavra – the

Kiev Monastery of the Caves, and the unfortunate Russian Solovetsky Islands, known as "Solovki", where the old monastery was turned into a cruel labour camp during Soviet times. There are also many pilgrimage sites to the north, the east and in the Far East, in India, Tibet, China, Korea, Japan, too many to list here.

∞∞∞

There are many testimonies to the exploits of sailors, to their daring and passion. Some sailors kept diaries, in which they described their adventures, recounted the breakages and shipwrecks they survived. But perhaps less is known about the sailors' discontent at sea, their restlessness and their joy when, after a long voyage, they caught sight of land. What kind of bread did they eat? What kind of flour was used – wheat, rye, barley? When and how did they light a fire and bake the bread on wood that was in short supply, or coal, which they didn't have? Which parasites – flies, worms, cockroaches, mice or rats – were the biggest threat to the provisions loaded on board before leaving, especially the ship's biscuit, which with each passing day became harder and drier, less tasty and harder to digest?

There are various testimonies about the bread sailors ate. Pliny the Elder called it *panis nauticus*. Unfortunately, the seventh volume of his *Naturalis Historia*, devoted to navigation (*de navigatio*), has been lost. It would undoubtedly have offered a good deal of information about bread. The *Odyssey* mentions "well-sewn skins" that were for containing bread and flour. The Greeks called the ship's biscuit *paxamida* or *dipyros* – twice toasted. In Hippocrates we find the term *dipyritesartos*. Describing the exploits of Cyrus, Xenophon writes: "We must, therefore, put up a sufficient quantity of food [bread], for without this we can neither fight nor can we live."

In the Middle Ages, bread differed from sea to sea, from port to port. On short "coastal voyages", known as "cabotage" (*cabotaggio*), one could bring some of the bread eaten at home in a bag or satchel. Longer voyages required large provisions of food. Big sailing ships, capable of crossing the Mediterranean and navigating the oceans, loaded up with both flour and wood, so that fresh bread could be made below deck, somewhere astern, at least for the captain and officers. As for the ordinary sailors, they nibbled pieces of the same ship's biscuit, day after day.

Documents found in the archives of harbour masters, shipbuilders and shipowners give us an idea of what the crew had for food. There are more similarities than differences in the instructions and rules prescribed by the administrations in Venice and Genoa, in Spain, Portugal, France and the Netherlands, and especially in the British Royal Navy, whose archives contain a large number of documents and records. In Venice the authorities preserved numberless edifying documents. The Senate adopted regulations and designated officials specifically charged with ensuring their implementation. The Republic of St. Mark sometimes gave cereals the generic name of *biada*. All of the Navy's provisions for the crew used to be called *panatica* – named after bread. On galley ships, "condemned" oarsmen were distinguished from those who received modest compensation for their labour in the form of food or money: the former were given 1lb 8oz of ship's biscuit a day (around 700g); the latter were given another pound on top of that. The many bakers around Venice's Arsenal had to obey the *regulae*, and numerous governors, *provveditore*, oversaw not only the production of the ship's biscuit (*provveditore del biscotto*) but also how it was protected against pests. The condemned, who were chained to the row locks, would sometimes be given bread made with carob flour. Carob makes one's stool hard and dry, and therefore easy to sweep off the deck without having to unchain the condemned oarsman or worry about him trying to mutiny or escape. It was easy to collect and sweep the faeces into the sea, leaving the deck clean. The fish would swarm around and feed on it, whereupon the sailors would catch them in small nets or on hook lines, cook and eat them.

In some coastal places and islands administered by the Venetian authorities, pensioners received a special supplement in the form of food, especially bread. This kind of subsidy was also given to under-age children after the death of their parents. The arrival of a ship, the unloading and distribution of bread, however modest the amount, was always an exciting event for the crowds. Perhaps nothing is awaited with such impatience as bread, even if it is just ship's biscuit.

Archive records include complaints against captains and their seconds in command, accusing them of having purchased poor-quality provisions – especially flour, grain and ship's biscuit – and then billing the authorities and shipowners for more than they had paid, pocketing the difference. It made some of them rich enough to be able build themselves palaces along the Canal Grande. So important was the quality of the bread to the crew that Genoa's bakers had to take an oath that they would deliver ship's biscuit that was "good and proper" – *bonus et ideoneus*. Whoever disobeyed would usually be punished.

Small maritime republics and big port towns along the Mediterranean followed the maritime rules and example of *La Serenissma* as far as it suited them. In the fifteenth century the city of Ragusa (Dubrovnik) built a huge storehouse, *Rupe*, for the grains arriving in their port from all over: from the Elafiti islands of Šipan, Konavle and Popovo Polje; from Albania; and sometimes also from the markets of a town that in Dalmatia is called *Jakin*, but we know as Ancona, in Italy. The Ragusa senate decided to build new granaries in nearby Ston. Part of the grain and flour was kept in storehouses known in the local dialect as *fundike*, taken from the Venetian *fondaco*. Made with wheat, barley, millet or sorghum flour, Ragusan biscuits, known locally as *beškoti*, were very popular. The bread made at the foot of the mountain above the city, Srđ, was often destined for sailors. The better-off would take *luk* (small, round, arc-shaped loaves), decorated with a sprig from the laurel or olive tree, or they would choose *škanatica*, a pie made with choice wheat flour, or the flat *teharica*, made for Easter, all of which were on offer at the town market and in front of the Church of St. Blaise, the city's patron saint, under the watchful eye of the women selling them, sometimes called *pancocolae*. The hierarchy had to be respected. Bread with seven crusts was reserved for the inmates of Ragusa's famous prison, known as Carmen, a corruption of Notre Dame du Carmel. Sailors of all nationalities would come to get their provisions of bread from Ragusa's granaries, made with wheat flour from the *fundike*.

Dubrovnik's older inhabitants still remember today the *beškoti* from nearby Brgat. Both the Grand and the Small Council of the tiny Republic made sure that the population was supplied with quality bread. They managed to save the people from famine but not from the plague.

Before setting sail from Palos in Spain, Christopher Columbus' three caravels loaded all the things that were needed for their voyage to the Indies. They then stocked up some more in the Canary Islands. Prominent on the list of foodstuffs were flour, wine and biscuits (*harina, vino y bizcocho*), along with drinking water and wood. In a letter addressed to the Crown of Castile, the explorer also mentions ship's biscuit. He issued an order for the storage hold – *cambusa* – to be locked while they were at sea. The ship's logbook shows that food was a constant concern on their long voyage. As he approached the first island he encountered, which he christened San Salvador, he saw a canoe full of native people rowing towards his ship, the *Santa Maria*, and compared their oars to "bakers' paddles". Such a comparison could only have occurred to the captain of three ships who, like his crew, was hungry for bread. He also spotted the "little loaves, no bigger than a fist" made by the locals, although he did not know how and with what ingredients they were made. The desire for bread is reflected in a letter written by Bartolome de Las Casas on 15 October 1492 to "Don Fernando and his wife Isabel, by the grace of God King and Queen of Castile, Aragon, Sicily and the Canaries". The sailors carried out the Admiral's orders and gave "bread and molasses" to the first man to step out of the canoe and onto their ship.

After sailing around Africa and reaching the real India, Vasco da Gama's crew arrived at the port of Calcutta. They offered the inhabitants greeting them at the pier loaves of bread as a token of friendship. In return, the locals gave them rice cakes sweetened with honey. Although bread was not unknown in this part of the world, the people preferred rice.

Food shortages were inevitable when sailing the vast waters of faraway seas. The Journal of Antonio Pigafetta, who accompanied Magellan on his expedition, gives a faithful account of the explorer's discoveries and tells us of the sufferings they endured while crossing the Pacific. The crew were unable to get any kind of fresh food for "three months and twenty days" and were obliged to eat old, mouldy ship's biscuit that had turned into powder, was crawling with worms and reeked of rat pee.

Such conditions were ripe for the spread of scurvy. It was the bane of both ordinary sailors and the ship's officers. The face and chest became bloated, the kidneys and thighs swollen, the muscles lax. The swellings, which were "hard as wood" and "grey as lead", oozed a pinkish pus. Teeth fell out of purulent gums and the tongue became hard. In his book *Geography* written in 7 BC, the Greek geographer, philosopher and historian Strabo described a similar disease that struck the expedition of the Roman prefect Gaius Aelius Gallus on its voyage to Egypt. The Dutch were probably among the first to use the term scurvy; in Italian, it is called *male delle gengive*, "gum disease". Perhaps that is one of the reasons why it is believed that the expression "bread with seven crusts" was coined by sailors.

The explorer James Cook also worried about food on the vessels he commanded, especially when in Plymouth he had to disembark more than 100 of his men who were afflicted with scurvy. The Royal Society in London joined up with the British Admiralty to try to find a remedy for the nasty disease and thus save the reputation of the Royal Navy. In France, Jean-Baptiste Colbert, the minister of finance, introduced a new measure: on longer voyages: vessels had to stop at particular ports to take on board fresh provisions, especially flour, ship's biscuit and bread. The Venetians, Spaniards and Portuguese adopted similar measures, each in their own way. These changes must have introduced some welcome novelties into the monotonous life of sailors. While in port, they could entertain themselves not only at the table but elsewhere, as well. As a result, some ports, long considered secondary, gained in importance. Ship's biscuit – whether it was called *biscotto, bicuit, bizcocho* or *beškot* – was already popular in Venice and Genoa, in Ravenna, Ragusa, Kotor, Bari and Ancona, and now also became so in major port cities like Marseille, Barcelona, Naples, Amalfi, La Rochelle and Bordeaux, in Smyrna, Piraeus, Haifa and Alexandria, in Cadix, Amsterdam, Odessa, Plymouth and who knows where else. Its quality and storage life varied from port to port. In the early nineteenth century, in 1821 to be exact, what could be called a miracle occurred in Crete, once the Kingdom of Candia: the discovery of a ship's biscuit made 152 years earlier at Venice's Arsenal. Carefully wrapped in sacks of jute, it had lost neither its shape nor its taste, only the colour was darker, of course; but it was not crumbly.

Many believe that ship's biscuit was called *galetta*, because its shape was reminiscent of a galley ship. However, the real origin is the word *gal*, which is of Celtic origin and came via Provençal to the shores of the Mediterranean; it is preserved in the French diminutive *galet* (a smooth stone, a pebble). The *gallettas* eaten by the ship's crew were indeed as hard as stone, and were shaped like the round polished stones one can find on the beach. That is how they got their name.

An old ship log records an unusual method used by experienced sailors to judge the quality of a ship's biscuit: they checked whether it took a sharp knock of the knuckle or a mallet to break it.

With the appearance of large vessels, first steam ships and then even bigger transoceanic liners, the food on board changed. The crews had big ovens at their disposal, enough wood and coal, flour, salt, yeast and whatever was needed to make bread that was worthy of the name. It replaced the ship's biscuit, flatbread, breadsticks, pretzels and even the Sardinian *pane carasau*.

But that is another part of the story, distinct from the one we wish to tell about the bread eaten by seafarers.

◊◊◊

The bread of soldiers has more than one thing in common with that of sailors: both are hard and both are bland. But the differences outweigh the similarities. It was nevertheless easier to obtain flour on land than at sea. Armies pillaged grain and the authorities collected it as a tax. On big campaigns, the generals brought along bakers for their soldiers. As for those troops, it was no easier for the soldier than it was for the sailor. For both, bread was not just food; it often provided consolation, as well. Perhaps the most democratic story of military bread is the story of the traditional bread of the Persian army from the eleventh century onwards.

Each soldier carried a small quantity of pebbles with him as he marched, and these were collected at camp to form the "sangak oven" that would bake the bread for the entire army. The large slabs of flatbread pitted with the indent of the pebbles were often eaten with lamb kebab.

Every language has a special term for "ammunition bread", the bread distributed to armies in times of peace and times of war. The Romans called it camp bread, panis castrensis. In every army, the official terminology, meant to guarantee obedience, is accompanied with an everyday vocabulary, which sometimes has humorous undertones. In Central Europe, and especially in the Austro-Hungarian Empire, soldiers carried in their knapsack or backpack a piece of bread called *komis* (ear-shaped). Sometimes, especially at the front, it was heavy, weighing somewhere between a ship's biscuit and an ordinary loaf of bread. In certain places they called it *cwibak* or *cibok*, and in Hungarian *cipó*. The troops did not eat the same bread as the squadron leaders, nor did the squadron leaders eat the same as the officers, or the officers the same as the generals. The ordinary soldier was often served *panada*, a kind of bread soup consisting of bread crusts and crumbs, with hot, salted water poured over it to make it more edible. The bread a soldier carried in his knapsack could be eaten with anything except gunpowder.

Life behind bars was always worse than military service, and subsisting on bread and water was not easy. The water was tepid and stale, the bread dry and tasteless. Some prisoners lived on bread and water for ten years and more. "Prison bread" has been common to all languages for as long as prisons have existed. In the gaols of Venice, especially in Piombi where Casanova was held, the bread given to prisoners was called "St. Mark's bread", after the patron saint of the city and the Republic. In French prisons it was sarcastically called "king's bread" (*pain de roi*) as the cost of the meagre portions was covered by His Majesty's coffers. To be sentenced to "bread and water" meant the same thing in all languages: prison.

And a "life sentence" was sometimes a fate worse than death.

From time immemorial, beggars have always asked for "a crust of bread" or a penny to buy "a morsel of bread". They differ in age, background and dress, and in whether they beg out of need or habit, whether they have no choice or have chosen begging as a profession. In ancient Greece, "cynics" were part of a school of thought aimed at defending freedom of speech while preserving complete independence by choosing to live on the street, begging. They roamed around the world "like dogs" (*kynos*), hence their name. They slept wherever they could lay their head, often outdoors, under a tree, or in a barn. Ignoring the stares of passers-by, they made love in public places. Diogenes is remembered, among other things, for the barrel he lived in, the dog that kept him company, the lamp that lit the way for him day and night, and the rags he wore. Antisthenes carried a staff in one hand and a satchel over his shoulder. He was famous among the cynics for hurling stinging jibes at his contemporaries. Their discourse, *parresia*, spared no one, not even Plato or Aristotle. They lived on the food that, despite everything, they managed to beg from their fellow-citizens. In fact, they condemned themselves to live, in the name of honesty, on bread and water.

In Christian times, the Gospel according to Luke describes poor Lazarus, "full of sores and desiring to be fed with the crumbs which fell from the rich man's table; moreover the dogs came and licked his sores." There are a number of poor mendicant religious orders: the Franciscans, "grey friars", who followed the example of St. Francis of Assisi, and notably among them the "barefoot friars"; the Dominicans, sometimes called the "black friars"; the Carmelites or "white friars"; and the Augustinians. The Council of Lyon, convoked in the thirteenth century, recognized these four as mendicant orders. Dervishes, especially the Mevlevis in Turkey, begged while whirling until they dropped in a religious trance that combined dance and prayer. They were content to be rewarded with "a morsel of bread".

Some old cities have preserved the custom of designating places where alms can be left, or "bread for the poor". In Venice, not far from the St. Samuel Church, in the niche of a wall in the narrow *Calle delle Carozze*, there is a box with a small metal door and inscribed above it are the words: *pane per i poveri*. There have always been good souls who come and leave a bit or bread here. In the Dalmatian city of Split, there used to be a similar box by the Silver Gate, near Diocletian's palace. Who knows if it is still there or if someone removed it, for there are fewer and fewer people who give bread to the poor, and there are more and more poor hungry for bread, a cynic might say.

In the preface to the anonymous *Liber vagatorum* ("Book of Vagabonds and Beggars"), Martin Luther castigated charlatans, who, having "made a pact with the devil" and profiting from his help, prevented bread from coming into the hands of real beggars, those who begged out of pure necessity.

You are not born a beggar, you become one. And you mostly do not become one of your own volition. Begging is an admonition to society and to religion: that society should ensure there is bread for everyone, and that religion should ensure no one is forgotten.

Some countries still have laws stipulating where and when begging is allowed, and where and when it is prohibited, while the beggars themselves find the best spots by a church, a mosque, in a square, a souk. Not all the blind are visually impaired nor are all the afflicted disabled. Some began begging as children, others when they were older, and others still in old age. Some were in their mother's arms when they first heard the words "bread, please", and tried to say it themselves. Whatever they asked for afterwards, they never forgot the word. *The Threepenny Opera*, dedicated to beggars, has already been written. It would be presumptuous to add anything to it.

∽∽∽

In some regions, the majority of beggars are Roma, a people who never enjoy the same privileges as the majority population. Their way of life is neither prohibited nor prevented, but it often arouses suspicions and is sometimes punished. No one knows exactly what the global Roma population is; in Europe they number perhaps 10 million. All together they outnumber the entire population of some countries and they are more numerous in some places than in others, but their number seems largest in the Balkans. Many more live their lives "on the road", coming and going from who knows where, their reasons for travel never known to us. Some have a sense of their native land, but not a homeland. They are a people dispersed, not a nation, nor a national minority, either, for they are "transnational". They do not have their own territory, government or army. Their dwellings are mostly not houses. They came to Europe following the sun, moving from east to west. As they crossed Persia, Armenia, Anatolia, they saw how local people made bread, though it must be said that it was not unknown to their ancestors, somewhere in ancient India or in the Far East.

History has not been kind to the Roma. They barely managed to preserve their name. In some places they were, and still are, called Manush, Sinti, Gitans, or Gypsies. Historically they served the community by forging everyday objects that are now obsolete, repaired cauldrons that are not in use anymore, shoed horses for carriages that are not driven anymore, made saddles, reins and belts for horsemen who don't ride anymore. They taught bears how to dance in public squares that have no place for them anymore. Their music and song filled cafés, where now there is the noise of machines. "Come, Gypsy, sing and chase away my sorrows" is still remembered in parts of the Balkans that do not reject "Balkanness".

Does anyone today remember that it was the Roma who instilled soul into the flamenco, Russian romance songs and Hungarian dances like the famous *csárdás*? That it was perhaps they who brought to Europe the old, rusty *cimbalom*, the probable precursor of the harpsichord and then the piano? Young Roma sang, danced and played the tambourine and pot drum. They charmed, read palms and told fortunes to earn money so that they could give bread to their children, husbands, lovers. Yet history and fate were cruel to the Roma.

The Holocaust didn't spare them, either.

There were more Roma in my home country of the former Yugoslavia than in neighbouring regions, and I sometimes spent time with them. They did not go to school, but I learnt a good deal from them. We don't know if their wanderings bring them happiness, but they certainly know how to lighten the load of unhappiness, even when living in a tent. It was my Rom friend that helped me to learn and record some of the things about their bread that I mention in this book.

He told me that the Roma have several words for bread: the most common is *marno*, followed by *manro, maro, mahno*. Flour is *arho* – maybe it's no accident that this noun has no plural in their language. Yeast is *humer*. *Bok* means hunger and *bokhalo* hungry – words one often hears in their presence. *Chalo* is to be full, *panif* is water, *jag* is fire, *lonm* is salt. To eat is *hav*, combining the present tense and the imperfective aspect, confusing grammar and reality. Surrounded by so much and deprived of everything, they make a distinction between what is pure, *vujo*, and impure, *mariame*, not only regarding food, but also in customs and human relations. Historically, they do not have written food recipes, and this includes for the making of bread, but their oral tradition is reliable, passed down word for word from one generation to the next. Their peripatetic way of life does not allow them to use an oven, but their biscuits can be also cooked on a stone and their bread on the embers of a fire. Both are tasty.

Their sayings about bread are full of wisdom. I have written some of them down here in the original, for the sound of the language, followed by the translation:

Kana bi e chorke marena marnesa, vov bi lengo vast chumidela.

"If you hit a poor man with a loaf of bread, he'll kiss your hand."

O marno shai so o Develni kamel thai so o thagar nashtisarel.

"Bread can do what neither God nor the tsar can."

Kana bi ovela ne phuo marno savorenge, chuche bi ovena vi e khangira vi e krisa.

"If there were bread enough for everyone on this earth, the churches and courtrooms would be empty."

Te si marne thei nai biuzhe, na bi trebela rudjipe.

"If there were more bread and fewer scoundrels, prayer would no longer be necessary."

O bokhalo dikhel suno e marne, o barvalo dikhel suno pe sune.

"The hungry dream of bread, the rich dream their dreams."

A young Rom woman with an infant in her arms, recited for me, in her language and then in translation, a short verse from a song about bread. It is called Marno:

I vogi e yag djuvdarel, / i pani o arko baidarel. / O humer i dai londiarel / thai peske ilesa gudliarel, / gudlo thai baro te ovel, / pire chkhavoren te chaliarel.

"Breath revives the fire,/ water expands the flour./ Mother, salt the dough/ and sugar it with your soul/ to make the bread sweet and rich,/ for it to feed the children.

While she was speaking, the child was quiet, looking around, as if participating in the recitation.

The Roma do not have fields to work. Today it is sometimes easier for them to beg and maybe even pilfer something from among the unnecessary items that fill our society. Tomorrow it may not be. "Maybe, but ... you know how that song goes: 'A Gypsy's sorrow never ends.'" That was the answer I got from an old Rom from my neck of the woods.

∞∞∞

Bread has always been kept in a special place: in the pantry, wrapped in a cloth to keep it fresh; in a linen or jute sack; in a straw or wicker basket; in the bundle of a traveller or the satchel of a pilgrim; in the knapsack of a soldier or the rucksack of a hiker; in the lap of a mother and wife, daughter and daughter-in-law. The Hebrews had many ways of preserving it in their ancient lands and during their migrations, keeping the leavened separate from the unleavened bread so as not to mix them or mistake the one for the other. The ancient Egyptians entrusted their bread to the darkness and silence of the pyramids for the afterlife. In keeping with Christian tradition, from ancient times to the present day, bread adorned the altar and was present in the tabernacle; it was placed in the ciborium of Catholics and on the paten of Eastern Orthodox believers; it was represented at the Last Supper and mentioned in pagan agapes. Carved into the stone walls lining the streets that lead to the Kaaba are nooks in which thin biscuits are still left for the *hadjis* who need something to restore their strength.

Grains, too, were carefully kept and stored: in granaries, attics, silos, under the decks of ships, under tarpaulins covering carts, and in all sorts of other places that were dry, protected, safe and well-guarded. Seeds required special attention to make sure that they did not germinate too soon or too late and were kept for the sowing season, with the promise of a good harvest.

The work of millers and bakers often exposed them to dangers and discomfort. It is no wonder, then, that they sought to surround themselves with patron saints, who, despite their number, were not always of help. The patron saints of bakers were St. Honoré of Amiens, St. Albert of Louvain, San Lorenzo *dei Fornai* of Florence, St. Elizabeth of Hungary (*Erszebet*), and St. Christina of Tyre, a martyr killed at the age of ten in the third century BCE. Millers have also placed their fate in the hands of St. Florian of Noricum, the virgin and martyr St. Catherine of Alexandria, St. Christina, St. Paul of Verdun and in some regions also St. Michael.

Emmer

Corn

Rice

Wheat

Barley

Rye

Millet

Oat

V.
SEEDS

Want and need called for ever-newer, ever-better varieties of grain. Selected for their quality and their yield, they were carried and harvested from one region to the next. Who were the first to carry seeds between regions, and why? Their names have been lost to the mist of time. We simply do not know their motivation or if they were following someone's orders.

Birds, too, carry seeds over long distances in their beaks, and afterwards the wind then scatters them in the surrounding valleys. Origin and destination are close and connected one minute, and far apart and distant the next. The grains brought from the east and the south contributed to a huge growth of the population in the west and north, to the benefit especially of Europe.

Bread changed the fate of countries and peoples.

The seed lies inside the grain and gives it its name. Cereals belong to the family of grasses and the soil, sun and water help them to sprout, grow and mature. They are mentioned in the Holy Scriptures: "Take thou also unto thee wheat, and barley, and beans, and lentils, and millet, and fitches, and put them in one vessel, and make thee bread thereof, according to the number of the days that thou shalt lie upon thy side, three hundred and ninety days shalt thou eat thereof." Thus spake Ezekiel.

Wheat was cultivated with special care. Its stalk is straight and tall, it has leaves, "spikelets" and a protective "beard" of bristles or awns around the husks of grain; the last leaf is known as a flag leaf. When it is threshed, the edible part of the grain is loosened from the chaff. The remaining wheat straw is used for many things: as floor and roof matting and fuel for the bread oven. Braided, weaved or twined, it is used to make baskets, mats and hats.

Over time, different varieties of wheat have been crossbred, adding to and changing each other, all with a view to improvement. Winter wheat is sown in the autumn, spring wheat in March or April. Both need quite a lot of sun, humidity and also peace and quiet. Mature wheat is a rich golden colour. Its flour, both "soft" and "hard", is white. Fertility goddesses decorated their shoulders, brows and breasts with ears of wheat. Conquerors and rulers did the same. Certain varieties of wheat were given female names: Aurora, Ceres, Victoria.

One often forgets that rice is a cereal, too. In the Far East, it replaced wheat, barley and rye, proving itself to be plentiful and soon growing everywhere. Once present it never entirely disappears, yet you won't find it on dry earth. More than any other cereal it needs water to grow. Though its roots do not run deep, they are widely spread out. The ear of rice is divided into several tillers, each of which bears a terminal flowering head. The more fruitful the ear of rice, the lower it droops. Rice grows quickly and produces several yields a year. The ears of rice are picked, not cut. Not all varieties are white – some have to be hulled, rinsed and cleaned for them to attain the white colour.

Many consider rice to be the best substitute for bread, especially in regions where there is not enough bread.

Barley is another old cereal. Originally from Africa, it is similar to, and often confused with, wheat – though its ears are darker. Once it is heavy with grain, it droops down almost to its roots, as if wanting to thank the soil that sustains it. Its grains are roundish on the top and tapered at the bottom. White barley, known as pearl barley, is obtained by stripping off the husk. Barley is resistant to blight and stem or "black" rust. Its flour is one of the main ingredients of wholemeal bread – a tribute to its strength and rustic nature. There are different varieties of barley, one of which is called distichon because of its two rows of spikelets. It is used with hop to brew beer.

Roasted and ground, barley can even replace coffee.

In times past, many of the fields of Anatolia, east Africa and southern Europe grew rye. Resistant to the cold, this cereal spread to the northern countries, where it acclimatized, and even succeeded at an altitude of more than 3,000-odd feet (around 1,000m). Its greyish-green grain is firm and oblong, and its stem thin, with small, elongated leaves. Flour made from rye is darker than wheat and barley flour. When kneaded into dough it goes well with cumin and dill. It is used to make bread sticks and crackers. Its bran has curative properties and is good for the circulation, blood pressure and digestion. Some naturalists believe that rye is older than barley, though there are also contrary views. Archaeological digs seem to support the one when they are not supporting the other.

Religions blessed all types of barley. Paganism made no distinction between them.

Millet can be recognized by its appearance, touch and taste. Its inflorescence, which holds most of the grain, is covered with tiny pinkish flowers, which almost come as a surprise. Historians remind us that millet keeps well in attics and was invaluable in times of trouble and war. It saved the Venetians when they were under siege from the Genoans. It served as a substitute for meat during Great Lent. Millet was often used as feed for livestock in barns, canaries in cages and pigeons on rooftops. It was recommended to pregnant women to give them energy, prescribed to frail patients to reinvigorate them and distributed to exhausted soldiers to revive them.

Some less fanciful researchers believe that millet is older not only than rye and barley, but than all other cereals, as well. People knew of it and ground it with their teeth before the grindstone and pestle were even invented, indeed before the first bread was ever made. It is difficult to say for certain, but its seed most likely comes from the Far East, from India, China or Korea.

Millet was supplanted by maize after the discovery of the New World, but it never disappeared.

Spelt fed the Romans before bread dough made its entrance into the Eternal City. Its grain was roasted on hot embers or boiled in water into a pottage called *puls*. Spelt is difficult to hull, because the hull sticks to the seed even when being ground. It is therefore easier to grind the hull than to try to remove it. One variety is called "big" spelt and the other "small" spelt. The difference is barely visible but nevertheless exists. Both germinate and grow in poor, unrewarding soil. Another advantage, perhaps, is that they are less affected by the cold than most other cereals.

Although mostly used as cattle feed, oats also deserve mention. They were not utterly unknown to the translator of the Holy Scriptures, St. Jerome, probably because they were given to goats in the region of Stridon, not far from the Adriatic coast where he was born. He left us with this brief comment: *Avena bruta pascuntur animalia / only brute beasts are fed with oats.* The grains of oats are tiny and difficult to hull. Some are long and sharp, and can be prickly; others are round and blunt, and harmless. When spilled onto a wooden board, they roll into small piles, like little pyramids. Perhaps it was this sight that once stoked the imagination of some pharaonic builder. What would the horsemen of ancient times and the Middle Ages have done if, in addition to rank grass and dry hay, they hadn't had oats to feed their horses? How would they have ridden across those vast expanses and conquered them? An oat bag and water bottle go together and complement each other. Oat groats were given to mothers breastfeeding their infants and are said to contain and give a "life force". They also protect the enamel of teeth.

When finely ground and roasted, oats can also be a substitute for coffee, especially in poorer countries.

Corn was brought across the ocean to us many thousands of years after the domestication of other cereals in Africa, Asia and Europe. Called "Indian wheat", "Spanish" and "Turkish" corn, it was long foreign to us before we fully adopted it. Cornbread, which does not take to yeast, enabled the New World to save the Old World. One should not forget that the Mediterranean survived thanks to this imported grain.

To grow corn, one does not have to plough very deep: it is content with a narrow furrow, grows quickly and in abundance. It has large, evenly distributed kernels on the cob. The cob itself is protected by green husks which, once they mature, suddenly pale in colour. Yellowish silky fibres protrude like tufts of hair from the tip of the ear of corn. Young corn, while it is still milky, is easy to roast on the embers of a fire. It is healthy and easy to digest. But when it is dry, it is hard to chew and the kernels get caught between the teeth. Corn porridge, or polenta, is often the food of the poor, but when artfully prepared, it can be found on the finest of dining tables.

Although cereals exist in all four corners of the world, there are regions where they are in short supply.

$$\Diamond\Diamond\Diamond$$

The words "seminary" and "seminar" come from the Latin *seminarium*, meaning seed plot, or breeding ground. Seminars took over the role once held by *symposions*, although they are meetings of very different natures. With his *Etymologiae*, St. Isidore of Seville (560-636) started a debate about the origin of words and things, but he did not discover where the names for certain grains came from. We may never find out what makes the biscuit called *ninda* in Sumerian different from the biscuit called *akala* in Akkadian or the Egyptian wheat *botet* different from the Babylonian *bututu*. In Sanskrit, the word *pa-yu* – as transcribed by scholars of the oldest idioms – means protector and guard. It lies at the root of the Latin words *panis* and *pater*: Bread protects and nourishes, and the father protects and nourishes in his own way. *Pastor, pascere* (pasture), the Russian *pishcha* (food), the Mideastern *pita*, and so many other kindred words all stem from the same root. The ancient Greek verb *paleomai* also refers to food and contains that same Indo-European seed. To the Romans, Jupiter –from *Jovis-pater* – was both father and protector. The Latin *parens* gave us *parent* in English and in other languages. By changing the first letter, pater became *Vater* in German and *father* in English, before being adopted by almost all Germanic languages. Latin and Romance derivations from the word *pane* give us compound words that link us to those with whom we share our daily bread, such as "companion" and "company", *compagnone, compagnie, compagno*, etc. All these examples show us just how far back these ancestries go.

Bread offers proof that is difficult to contest.

The Greek noun *artos* – bread that is made, kneaded – is derived from the verb *ararisko* ("to make or adapt something"). The word was already used in Hellenic literature by Homer, Pindar and Aeschylus, Socrates, Plato and Aristotle. Under the influence of "demotic", colloquial speech, a new noun appeared for bread: *psomos*. It comes from the word *psomizo* ("morsel, crumb"). The German *brot* and English *bread* are linked to the verbs *brauen* and *brew*: to brew like beer and ferment like dough, probably under the analogous influence of *brechen* and "break". These words are a marriage of want and desire. Bread was broken off piece by piece, eaten morsel by morsel, broken up crumb by crumb.

The proto-Germanic and paleo-gothic words *hlaibaz, hlaifs* in Old English and *hljeb* in Old Slavonic, also share a common root, linked to the ancient Greek word *klibanos* ("a cooking receptacle"), initially made of clay, and later metal. In ancient Rome, a soldier wearing armour was called a *clibanarius*. Across the Channel, *hlaifs* became first *hlaf* and then loaf, only to become part of composite words such as *hlafweard* and *hlaford*, designating he who has bread, he who masters it, eventually leading to the word *lord*. *Lady* stems from hlæfdige, taken from the root *hlaf* and the verb *dig* (to knead). Thus, the ladies of proud Albion had the honour of bearing the title "kneaders of bread".

The road from a clay or metal receptacle to armoured soldier and finally to the title of lord was a long one. When capitalized, lord is also the Lord. The Last Supper, where Christ broke and distributed bread, is also known as the Lord's Supper.

All Slavic languages adopted the same word for bread – probably through ancient Gothic, Old German or Balto-Slavic – *hljeb*, pronounced and written in various ways: *хлеб, hljeb, хлиб, hlib, леб, lib*, etc. However, in Croatian and Slovenian, where the word *hljeb* is not unknown, bread is commonly called *kruh*. Sometimes a distinction is made in these languages between bread and its form: *hljeb kruha* is used for "a loaf of bread". The expression was especially prevalent in Podravina, a region of Croatia well known for its naïve art, and particularly for the school of naïve painters based in the village of Hlebine, whose name has a clear connection with bread. The Slavic root *hlaib* or *hlaibaz* stems from the Indo-European *glei* (*glebh*). In various Romance languages it means a clod of earth (*glaeba, gleba, glèbe*). The word *globe* shares the same root.

The word *kruh*, which exists in several Slavic languages, also meant a piece, a fragment, a crust, similar to *psomi* in the demotic or Greek. In poorer regions and communities, bites of bread were slowly chewed, morsel by morsel. The loaf, *hljeb*, was not cut, it was *broken*, and so it was *krhak*, fragile, and therefore called *kruh*. Perhaps this change of name was encouraged by the Christian tradition of breaking bread or by the Eucharistic rite. The word *skrušenost* (*s-kruš-enost*, "contrition"), is rooted in the word *kruh*.

And so seeds take us from the earth (*glèbe*) to the Earth, from the clay receptacle to the bread in which it is baked, from paternity to divinity.

The French *fouace*, a traditional bread, comes from the Greek, through the Latin and the root in Romance languages that designates the place where one makes a fire – *phogo*, focus, *focolare*, etc. The Italian *focaccia* crossed the Adriatic and established itself in the Balkans and Eastern Europe under the Slavic name *pogača*. It has the same root as the Provençal *fouasse* (or *fougasse*), the pride of Montpellier, Narbonne, Nice and especially Marseille. It holds its own against many of France's better-known breads such as the *baguette, bâtard, ficelle, pain d'epices, pain de mie,* or *pain de campagne.*

Etymologies reveal the importance and power of seeds. Let us therefore take this opportunity to pay tribute to St. Isidore of Seville, and his early seventh-century etymological encyclopaedia.

∞∞∞

In ancient times, certain ceremonies provided occasion to spread the benefits of bread; they were *seminars* in the true sense of the word. Rulers and their subjects, sometimes even slaves, would take part. In ancient Egypt the biggest pharaonic celebration was *Heb-Sed,* at which loaves of fresh flatbread would be handed out to the people, and then *liquid bread* – beer – would be poured over them. Even the power of Ramses II was associated with a good harvest, as celebrated in these words: "Wherever your sandals step, the harvest is plentiful."

The pagan *Odyssey* also says: "Stranger or suppliant stands in a brother's place to any man who has a touch of good feeling." In its turn, the Old Testament blessed the virtue of hospitality. "God loves the stranger and giveth him bread … and thou shalt love him as thyself, for ye were strangers in the land of Egypt … And when thou shalt have reaped corn in thy field, and shalt have forgotten a sheaf in thy field, thou shalt not return to take it; it shall be for the stranger, and the orphan, and the widow, that the Lord thy God may bless thee in all the works of thy hands." In the shade of the oak tree of Mamre, Abraham met three travellers in front of his tent: "And I will fetch a morsel of bread, and comfort ye your hearts; after that ye shall pass on." He asked Sarah to "make ready quickly three measures of fine meal, knead it, and make cakes upon the hearth." He did not know that standing before him were three angels. Because he shared this bread, Abraham became the symbol of hospitality in Judaism, in Christianity and in Islam, where he is called Ibrahim.

In ancient Israel, the Law and rites determined the days that were especially marked by prayer, forgiveness and sharing. The festivals, *Yom Tovim,* were important events in the Jewish calendar. For centuries, *Yom*

Kippur, considered the Shabbat of Shabbats, has been celebrated each year, as have the festivals of *Shavuot* and *Sukkot,* both connected to agriculture, and *Pesach,* Passover. On the second day of *Pesach,* a measure (*omer*) of grain is to be taken to the Temple for the "loaves of proposition" (*lehem ha-panim*). *Shavuot* announced the beginning of the barley harvest and *Sukkot* marked the end of all the year's harvests. In between these main festivals were the days of *Chol Hamoed,* which permitted lighter chores, such as kneading dough and making bread. Deuteronomy 14:25 says: "Then,shalt thou go unto the place which the Lord thy God shall choose." And that place was Jerusalem, initially. After the Temple was destroyed, pilgrimages were made to Shiloh and the sanctuaries of Dan and Bethel. In each of these places and on each occasion, a special unleavened bread was made and offered.

Ancient Greece celebrated pan-Hellenic and pan-Athenian festivals every four years in Delphi and Olympia, and every other year in Isthmia and Nemea. Other celebrations were of regional or local importance, but all included *rhapsodoi* and *kitharodoi,* dance and song, music and poetry recitals. Contests were held, sacrifices offered, plays performed. The winners received a wreath, awards and applause. The central venue of the celebrations, the Pompeion, was built on the outskirts of Athens. The Hippodrome in Piraeus and the theatre of Dionysus at the foot of the Acropolis were open to all citizens. People came and went from all over. The celebrations in a way resembled banquets or *symposions,* though they were not exactly the same. On some occasions, the people, *demos,* took an active part. Bread thus became an expression of, and at times the guarantee of democracy.

Rome was not without festivals of its own. The *Saturnalia* were held at the end of the year to celebrate the mythical rule of Saturn, the golden age of Latium. The *Neptunalia* were a similar festival, under another name. The *Tiberinalia,* as the name suggests, were held on the banks of the river – *in portu Tiberino* – whose waters refreshed the summer evenings and late-night trysts. The *Portunalia* celebrated Portunus, the god of gates and harbours. (Varron called him: *deus portuum portarumque praeses*). The *Cerealia* began in the spring, in honour of Ceres, the goddess of fertility and grain. "Ceres was the first to dig up the ground with the curved ploughshare" (*Prima Ceres unco glebam dimovit aratro*), writes Ovid in *Metamorphoses*. Even before the first bread was made near the Capitol, let alone after, the city offered the people various "games" for entertainment: *ludi Megalenses* in honour of Cybele, *ludi Apollinares* in honour of Apollo, *ludi Romani* in honour of Jupiter, *ludi Plebeii*, the "plebeian games", open to all citizens, and *ludi Florales*, a riot of flowers and fragrances. Bread was celebrated with Fornax, the goddess of ovens, who gave her name to *Fornacalia*, an ambiguous ceremony, perhaps one of a kind. It can be assumed that everything has already been said about Rome's taste for "bread and games" – *panem et circenses*. Horace liked to say that it is good to go mad once a year. Ancient Rome offered more occasions than that once a year.

Later on, the Christian Church wanted to bring the protocol of ceremonies in tune with the paradigms of faith. It tried to synthesize the old pagan festivals, reconcile the Old Testament and the New, to rid itself of some of its Judaic heritage, to establish its own liturgy, to introduce its own preaching. It set the dates for celebrating the birth and resurrection of the Son of God, the birth and Assumption of the Virgin Mary, the day of the Pentecost and of the Holy Sacrament, of various saints whose example enriched and inspired Christianity.

The rite of the Eucharist was an occasion for bread and faith to meet and imbue each other.

∽∽∽

The more dangerous the journey, the greater the appreciation of the hospitality offered to travellers. The Greeks extolled *philoxenia*. Jewish communities in the diaspora opened shelters near synagogues, called *Hachnasat Orchim* or "Welcoming Guests". In the Mediterranean world, *Pax Romana* guaranteed a certain degree of security. After becoming the official religion of the Roman Empire during the reign of Constantine, Christianity opened its doors to the stranger. St. Peter gladly followed

Abraham's example of welcoming strangers and pilgrims (*paroikoi kai parepidemoi*). Churches distributed letters of communion (*litterae communicatoriae*) to the faithful, recommending them to the care of monasteries and convents. Names like Martha and Marie, Simon, Lot, as well as Jesus himself, became symbols of Christian hospitality. The Council of Nimes, held at the end of the fourth century, did, however, warn the faithful to be vigilant and avoid awkward visitors – vagrants, thieves and the truculent.

In the Muslim world, pilgrims on their way to Mecca and the Kaaba were often greeted by the people of the desert and its oases, who gave them dates and cakes. Three surahs of the Quran – *Al Hidjr, Hud* and *Az-Zariyat* – refer to Ibrahim (Abraham) and how our common ancestor treated visitors. In Arabic he was given the name *Abu-ad-Dayfan* ("the father of hosts"). He received visits not only from ordinary travellers, *musafirs*, but also from *meleks* ("angels") or the messengers of God. The holy book of Islam calls a guest *daif*, and hospitality *ikram ad-daif*. The *Sahabi* Abu Hurairah, a companion of the Prophet, wrote in one of his *hadiths*: "Whoever believes in Allah and the Last Day, should serve his guest generously." To which Anas ibn Malik added that angels do not enter houses that do not welcome guests. Muslim countries saw the spread of *musafirhan*, a kind of guest house for travellers and strangers. To those who close their door to a stranger, the fourteenth surah of the Quran says: "The deeds of those who deny the existence of their Lord are like ashes blown about by a strong wind on a stormy day."

Although poorer than the other inhabitants of the desert, the Bedouins also saw hospitality as a duty. They did not write down their customs and laws, but they remembered and honoured them all the same. To them, guest and traveller were synonymous. They shared with them bread made of barley flour and sprinkled with sesame seeds. In his great poetic work *Masnavi (Mathnawi)*, Jalal ad-Din Rumi, better known simply as Rumi, wrote: "The Merciful (God) has implanted hospitality to strangers and entertainment (of guests) in the villagers ... Hospitality and entertainment (of guests) are characteristic of tent-dwellers ... Every day in the villages there is a new guest who has none to help him except God."

The *tariqa* dervishes of Anatolia adopted some of the habits of the old shamans, enhancing them with their own experience of fasting, and the bread that comes at the beginning and the end of a fast. The swirling dance of the dervishes always earned a loaf of bread as a token of gratitude. Sufis complimented the old rites with their own understanding of the relationship between body and soul. Their tables were modestly laid with just a soft, flat, usually unleavened roll made of barley or rye flour.

∞∞∞

When placed on the table still hot and fresh from the oven, bread heralds a kind of celebration of the assembled family: traditionally the mother who made it, the father who earned it and the children to whom it is offered. This domestic rite has both pagan and religious elements, but they are difficult to enumerate, let alone recount individually or collectively.

Preserved in a private collection in Sicily, an old text written by an anonymous chronicler – illegible in some places and ravaged by time in others – gives us a glimpse of the role bread played in certain celebrations on the island. It maintains that while the ceremonies' sacred aspects were intended to promote piety their secular aspects turned in a quite different direction. While both body and spirit were equally engaged, the physical often overpowered the spiritual. Participants in the ceremonies would move from the sanctuary to the public square, from Mass to street performance, from the religious procession to the public fair. The bread and wine consumed on these occasions made the events look like a walking *symposion*.

Bread was offered in all its shapes and sizes, different and similar at the same time.

During Holy Week, festivities were held all over Sicily, both along the coast and inland, with variations from place to place. Palermo and Montereale, Cefalù, Agrigente, Enna, Catania, Gela, Syracuse, Ragusa: every town lent something of its own to the celebrations. Scenes from the life of Christ and the Virgin Mary were performed both inside and outside the churches: the washing of feet, the Last Supper, on the Road to Calvary, *Ecce homo*, Deposition from the Cross (*a scisa a cruci*). The embroidered ornamentation on the garments (*addobbi*) reproduced the shapes of a loaf or cake (*marmurati*). Biblical figures passed by in the streets and squares as people dressed up as Mary, Magdalene and Veronica, Nicodemus and Joseph of Arimathea, Roman legionaries and Judaic dignitaries, priests and Pharisees, men in turbans and little girls in white dresses (*verginette*). Here and there one could detect different touches of Spanish, Genoan, Byzantine and, in places, Arab influence. The participants carried torches (*paramiti*) and lit fires along the way. And throughout the celebrations, bread was brought out, broken and distributed. It was both a daily and a festive bread.

Perhaps no other Mediterranean island has as many different kinds of bread as Sardinia. The tribes and ancient peoples that succeeded one another in the course of prehistory and history – the Sards, Nuraghes, Punics, Phoenicians and Phaeacians, both indigenous and newcomers – cultivated and worked the fields, sowed, reaped and ground grains, using them to make porridge, cakes and, last but not least, bread. Isolated from the world and current history, captives of the sea and their own destiny, they gave free rein to their imagination. Women seem to have been more involved in creating bread than their husbands, who were busy fishing and hunting, working the fields and farming. Anyone who steps foot in Sardinia, especially when St. Efisio is being celebrated, will hear unusual names and nicknames for bread, some of which are untranslatable: *civraxu, pintau, civargiu, tundu, loriga, coccoi, tureddu, jaos, cruxi, pane de lu preti, pane 'e sposos, pane di Sant Antonio, di Santa Rita, di San Giovanni,* and, perhaps the best known of them all, *pane carasau,* a thin, crisp flatbread. *Pane cafone* from Campania is not unknown in Sardinia, either, nor is the unsalted *pane sciocco* of Tuscany, nor the famous, impressive bread of Altamura, except here these breads are made in a different way and under a different name. The composition of and balance achieved between some of these breads may have their own metrics or prosody known only to those who make them. The island also has a special bread for bachelors and unmarried girls, and it is offered to guests at a festival called *la festa de is bogadius*. It used to be held in a place called Siurgus Donigala, near Cagliari. When the Church disavowed it in 1952, the stubborn islanders simply moved it to the town of Nuoro, which was obviously more willing to stretch the rules.

Until recently, some islands in the Ionian and Aegean, but also in the Adriatic and Tyrrhenian seas, held lavish wedding festivals. Sadly, they are becoming fewer and farther between. In Rhodes, Crete and Cyprus, pieces of bread are still tossed at newlyweds to wish them a long life and healthy progeny. In the town of Komiža, on the Croatian island of Vis, people used to make small bread rolls using carob flour. The islanders called them *hlipčići* or St. John's bread. Fallen crumbs would be carefully gathered and left for the sparrows, pigeons and seagulls to find.

But the people made sure that the pigeons did not chase away the sparrows nor the seagulls the pigeons.

In some places, they still make "bread for the dead" on days of mourning. This tradition is maintained more on certain Mediterranean islands, where the "justice of the stone" reigns (*la giustizia della pietra*, as the poet put it), than on the continent. In ancient times, Charon rowed the dead across the River Styx in a boat containing offerings of bread. This ancient tradition did not completely disappear with the advent of Christianity. The Council of Nicaea, held at the beginning of the fourth century, stipulated that "whoever is near death should not be deprived of the final and necessary Viaticum". However, the Council of Hippo advised Christians not to take the Eucharistic bread on such occasions.

Islam, like other faiths, commemorates in festivals key events in its past. Bread is always part of these occasions. Ramadan (called *Ramazan* in Turkey and the Balkans) is celebrated in the ninth month of the lunar year to commemorate when the Quran was first revealed to the Prophet Muhammad. The faithful fast for as long as there is daylight. When the sun sets, between *al-maghrib* and *al-isha*, the fasting is broken with *iftar*. The faithful are then given a soft flat roll to placate the empty stomach and prepare the body for the feast to come. The twenty-seventh day, the highlight of the Ramadan period called "The Night of Destiny" (*Laylat Al Qadr*), is the occasion when bread is placed on the table before any other food.

Another important celebration takes place in the last month of the year. In Arab countries it is called *Eid al-Adha*, and in Turkey and the Balkan countries *Qurban Bayram*. Following a tradition older than Islam itself, a sheep is sacrificed as a symbol of Ibrahim's willingness to sacrifice his only son. This sacrifice (*Nahr*) is accompanied by a prayer: *Allahu Akbar, Allahu Akbar, wa lillahil hamd*. The Prophet's birth is celebrated on the seventieth day of the year of the Hijri. Ashura, in the month of *Muharram*, marks the day that Hussein, the son of Ali, was martyred. This is when Shiite pilgrims make their way to Karbala, around 65 miles (100km) from Baghdad. During this period, the faithful are offered a multitude of breads and cakes, all stacked in a pile or strung on a cord: *khobz, aish, tharid, raghif, rakik...* They range in colour from white to a desert-sand grey, from amber to a browner hue, like the earth of the oasis.

Here, as elsewhere, the celebrations have long been a kind of seeding ground for bread.

Along with Islam, the Turks brought to the territories they conquered some of the customs of hospitality that they had picked up in the Middle East, the Maghreb, Mashreq and elsewhere. These traditions of *adet* have been preserved in the Balkans, and not only among its Muslim inhabitants. Even after the collapse of the Ottoman Empire, certain terms lived on, such as *nimet* – "favour" (from the Arabic *ni-mai*), also used for bread; *Božiji nimet* – "godsend"; *merhamet* (Arabic *marhama*) – "alms, charity"; *sevap* (Arabic *tawab*) – "pious deed"; *peshkesh* (Slavicized peščeš, of Persian origin) – a "gift or present"; *nafaka* (Arabic *nafaqah*) – "food, drink or some other form of charity that is given or received"; *mubarek* (literally: "congratulations") – a celebration observed with different foods, notably bread. *Zakat*, one of the five pillars of Islam, calls for giving grains, dates and bread to the needy. *Sadaka* (Arabic *sadaqa*) is a gift or alms that "extinguishes sin as water extinguishes fire", wrote imam An-Nawawi in one of his *hadiths*. *Zakat al-Fitr* (alms for the poor when breaking the fast) is given on the day of Eid al-Fitr, marking the end of Ramadan. It amounts to a little over 3 lb (around 1.5 kg) of wheat flour or, in its place, getting on for 7 lb (around 3 kg) of barley flour; if there is no flour then money can be given in its stead. Until the last war that tore apart the Balkans, these and similar words were used not only in Muslim but also in Christian families in various parts of Bosnia-Herzegovina, and in Kosovo, as well.

Unfortunately, some such words have fallen out of use in the region. The war silenced them; there was not enough "bread of hope and peace", to quote the poet.

Wherever you travel in Turkey, you will discover that people have an appetite for good bread, more secular, perhaps, than religious. Turkish military commanders reached the Mediterranean on horseback while ordinary soldiers came on foot: there were not enough carriages or horses to transport everyone, and even the roads were few and far between. The Turks had already cultivated grains in the regions they came from; they knew how to cook and grind them, but they did not yet use them for making bread. As they crossed various countries in Asia and part of Europe, Turkish armies discovered and tasted everything that could be made with cereals. They called bread *ekmek*, from the Turkish verb "to sow". Soon they expanded on that, giving other special names to bread: *biberli ekmek* – "peppery", *baharatli ekmek* – "made for Bayram", *setikli* and *tahinli ekmek* – "for other celebrations". *Somun*, of Persian origin, is a flat, round, softer and tastier bread than the ordinary variety. *Yufka*, a thin sheet of dough, usually made of wheat flour, is used for sweet and savoury pastries. It is known all over the Balkans, with the dough being "rolled out" into a sheet the Greek, Slav, Romanian, Albanian, Aromanian way, often on a sheet spread over the floor or across a large table using a long pole so that the pastry has to hang down on either side and is spread thinly. The story is, though it is difficult to prove, that a kind of crescent-shaped roll was first made at the foot of the ramparts of Vienna, which was under siege by the sultan's troops who were waving Ottoman flags bearing the Islamic crescent. It then made its way to Paris, where it conquered the world under the name *croissant*.

Jews who arrived in the Ottoman Empire and remained for a long time were more focused on preserving old customs than adopting new ones. The Ottomans welcomed the Sephardim with fewer prejudices than elsewhere. Consequently, in Thessaloniki, Smyrna and Sarajevo there was a wide variety of both Jewish and other breads. During the week of Passover, *matzah* was made as prescribed by the rabbis in the *Halakhah*: unleavened, crispy, quite different from *chametz*. "On the eve of Shabbat and during the days of Yom Kippur," wrote a Bosnian chronicler, "the smell of matzah, accompanied by silent prayer, wafted through the air from one end of Sarajevo-town to the other." The Sephardim called their shabbat bread *pitikas* in some places, and *challah* in others. It is thanks to them that the southern Slavs adopted a kind of cake known as *pan di Spagna* (*patišpanja*), whose first syllables the popular sense of humour changed to *pati* (suffer). And one must not forget the *Ha Lachma Anya*, the "bread for the poor", representing the "bread of affliction", served for Passover. Each of these breads had its own crust. One of them, according to a Sarajevo rabbi, was called the "crust around the heart".

∞∞∞

The collapse of the Ottoman Empire brought many changes to the old Turkish provinces, from Rumelia, which remained in Europe, to "Stambol on the Bosphorus" and its surroundings. It had its own "seminaries", in the sense that we mean here: the *Han, meyhane, konak, aşçılık, caravanserai* – they all changed their purpose and their names. *Pasha konak* near Constantinople disappeared, as did the wooden *han* on the hills of the Golden Horn. Once loud taverns gave way to new neighbourhoods, such as Tepebaşı, Cihangir, Zeyrek; built nearby were the palaces of Dolmabahçe and Yildiz, the hotels of Bebek Bay, the elegant buildings of Çukurcuma. There was a time when each of these *quartiers* made its own bread, and they competed with one another. The air was redolent with its aroma, and the bread itself evoked the scent of the past, the better part of the past.

In Central Europe, ancient towns became cities, and some cities came metropolises. They grew faster than the roads that connected them. In the winter, the snow made it difficult to move around, and some places became inaccessible and were left to their own devices. It was a time of religious and popular festivities, Christmas and New Year celebrations. Refusing to be imprisoned within its own confines, the imagination gave free rein to unusual expressions and surprising adventures. This gave birth, among other things, to a wide variety of breads of different shapes, sizes and colours. Indeed, nowhere else, perhaps, were there so many as here in Central Europe: *mischbrot, weizenbrot, roggenbrot, vollkornbrot, steinofenbrot, holzofenbrot* and many, many other different kinds, some of them with such curious names as *pumpernickel* or the famous *bretzel*; from small buns and rolls (*kipfel, semmel*) to the big *milchbrot* (renamed *milibrod* in some parts of the Balkans). And so it went from Vienna and Salzburg to Budapest, Prague and Bratislava, Zagreb, Ljubljana and Novi Sad in the Austro-Hungarian Empire and from Cologne to Munich and who knows how much farther north and south. Pastries followed in their wake, sometimes showing even more imagination than the bread itself.

It is not without reason that they became known as *viennoiseries*.

∾∾∾

The seeds and the kind of seminaries we're discussing here require, perhaps, a special semantics or semiology, if you will permit this play on words. Bread figures in sayings that bring together experience and wisdom. They comprise a kind of common man's encyclopaedia: "to earn one's bread and butter by the sweat of one's brow", "to eat white bread" in times of plenty and "black bread" in times of want, to beg for "a crust of bread", to "break bread" with someone, "bread is the staff of life", to "cast one's bread upon the waters", "one does not live by bread alone", ""half a loaf is better than no bread at all", "if you have bread, don't look for cake", to survive "on bread and water" in prison, "blessed bread" after communion,

"If your enemy is hungry, give him bread."

Bread has appeared in literature since the very beginnings of both. Psalm 104 blesses the "bread which strengtheneth man's heart". Ancient Greek choruses sang the praises of bread in dramas, tragedies and comedies. It is evoked in the dialogues of Euripides and Aristophanes. Aeschylus' Clytemnestra cries out against "the bread of slavery". Aristotle's *Rhetoric* distinguishes between "soft and hard bread" in life and morals. Plato's *The Republic* does not forget those who have only dry bread, yet still celebrate. Plutarch completes Euripides' thinking with: "Upon good hopes, exiles can thrive, they say ... It is sad to want, for Honour buys no bread."

Bread is also present in the Latin tradition, in both prose and poetry. In the *Aeneid*, Virgil extends his hand to he who "brings bread to his children". The *Annals* of Tacitus note that bread itself can be a reason for "dependence, slavery or luxury". Seneca uses a parable to depict the process of making bread: "water was sprinkled on the flour and by constant handling used to soften it and form bread" (*assidua tractatione perdomuiit finxitque panem*).

In modern times, too, we have described and extolled bread in works considered "more durable than brass". In *Il Convivio* ("The Banquet"), Dante says "blessed are the few who sit at that table where the bread of the angels is eaten". Nor does he forget the experience of exile, not even when approaching the Gates of Paradise: "Thou shalt learn how salty is the taste of other men's bread" (*Tu proverai si come sa di sale / Lo pane altrui*). For Petrarch, "water and bread are more important than ... gems". Writing about grains and seeds in one of his notebooks, Leonardo da Vinci observed a paradoxical situation: "Men will deal bitter blows to that which is the cause of their life (in thrashing Grain)." Or: "By sowing, does not man toss away his own provisions?" (*le proprie provviste*).

On an island that did not have an abundance of grain, English literature, especially with and after Shakespeare, did not overlook daily bread either. Richard II tasted "the bitter bread of banishment". Romeo and Juliet, in their passion, tasted "God's bread" that drives one mad. The great playwright also took every opportunity to mock the lowbrow "humour of bread and cheese". For Tennyson, bread is a guarantee of the truth: "I speak the truth, as I live by bread!" Bacon warned his compatriots, "Touch not the thievish breads of perverse doctrines." Alone on a desert island, Robinson Crusoe realized, distraught: "I neither knew how to grind or make meal of my corn ... nor, if made into meal, how to make bread of it."

Bread is not the child of solitude, even though fate often makes it so.

In his novel *The Betrothed*, Alessandro Manzoni bears witness to the revolt of the bread-starved poor. His novel rings with the cries of the French Revolution: "Bread! We don't need promises, we need bread and we need it now." Even before the revolution, people were publicly calling for the "bread of equality" (*pain d'égalité*). Millers and bakers were accused of starving the people. The patron saints of their trades were too weak to protect them from the fury of the crowds. Later, Victor Hugo raised his voice as both a republican and a writer, saying: "The theatre should make thought the bread of the crowds."

According to the poet and Christian Charles Péguy, "He who is too much in lack of daily bread no longer has any desire for bread everlasting." Just before committing suicide, Mayakovsky, the Soviet poet, playwright, artist, and actor, wrote to his beloved: "I simply ask for your body as Christians pray: 'Give us this day our daily bread.'" In one of his works, Apollinaire describes "polka loaves, like round coins, crusted with gold and silvered with powdered flour ... little Vienna rolls, like pale oranges..." When war brought poverty, the French poet Francis Ponge wrote a poem revealing the geography of bread: "The surface of bread is a marvel to behold, if only because of its quasi-panoramic aspect: as if one had the Alps, the Taurus or the Cordillera of the Andes under the hand."

The verse and song of the old harpist in Goethe's *Wilhelm Meister Lehrjahre* ("Wilhem Meister's Apprenticeship") became part of popular speech: "Who never ate his bread in tears / Who never through the mournful night / Sat weeping on his bed with fears / He knows not, heavenly powers, your might." More than one artistic German soul cursed his art – *eine brotlose Kunst* – an art that does not bring bread.

Mohamed Choukri, a writer of Berber origin and Arabic expression, retraces some painful memories in his autobiography *For Bread Alone*. A hungry and lonely child, he watched a fisherman eat bread, and then toss what was left into the water. He plunged into the water and grabbed it, clutching it in his hand ... a turd was floating right next to it. He ate first the one and then the other.

The twentieth-century Croatian writer Miroslav Krleža enjoyed listening to his grandmother and in *Djetinstvo u Agramu* ("A Childhood in Agram") he wrote her words down in the Croatian *kajkavian* dialect: "Peasant bread, not even a dog would lick it. But corn bread is tasty and thick, like a cake ... Military bread is sour and smells like a Home Guard's willy..." The Croatian poet Ivan Mažuranić spoke out in support of the Serbian and Montenegrin rebels who rose up against the Ottoman Empire: "Bread, bread, Sir. It's been a long time since we've seen bread." His compatriot, the poet Tin Ujević paid painful homage to the "bread of poison and bitterness".

Gibran Khalid, the Lebanese-born poet who spent almost all of his life in the United States, an Arab who wrote in English, spoke wisely about many things, including bread: "If you bake bread with indifference, you bake a bitter bread that feeds but half man's hunger." Both North and South America, the former in its frantic rat race and the latter in its poverty, have failed to pay attention always to the freshness and quality of bread. The writer Henry Miller warned his fellow-Americans in the twentieth century of the damage that bad bread can cause. In his essay "The Staff of Life" he wrote: "Poor bread ... bad teeth, indigestion, constipation, halitosis, sexual starvation, disease and accidents, the operating table, artificial limbs, spectacles, baldness, kidney and liver trouble..."

In today's world, which strives to be a "global village", bread – alas – is becoming increasingly dull.

"Bread? Bread is the one thing hermits do not have," said Zarathustra as penned by Nietzsche. Dostoyevsky seems to have adopted a similar tone: "Do you see these stones in this bare, scorching desert? Turn them into bread and mankind will run after you ... But you did not want to deprive man of freedom and rejected the offer, for what sort of freedom is it, you reasoned, if obedience is bought with loaves of bread."

There are so many common situations and experiences arising from difficulties over the fair distribution of bread across the ages. There are similarities, for instance, between the Roman Gracchi brothers, who tried to reform the production of grain and distribution of bread, and the French pharmacist and agronomist Antoine Parmentier, who recommended replacing cereals in regions where they were in short supply with potatoes or chestnut flour. One can link the ardent Roman gastronome Marcus Gavius Apicius and the way he used the military bread *bucella* in his sauces with the "transcendental gastronomy" preached by the now almost forgotten *maître* Brillat-Savarin. The latter proclaimed his neighbour, a baker who made bread for the Duke of Orleans and Prince of Condé, the "top bread-maker in the world". Both Apicius and Brillat-Savarin had something in common with Lord John Montagu, the fourth Earl of Sandwich, who lived in the eighteenth century. He loved to gamble and in order not to interrupt his games at the card table he would ask his servants to bring him slices of roast beef between two slices of bread. Thus the famous sandwich got its name. Gibbon mentions him with a certain note of reservation.

Once upon a time, visionary poets recognized in bread the sparkle of jewels and sunlight. May our daily bread glow on your "ruby (*yaqut*) lips" wrote the Persian poet Hafiz, who knew the whole of the Quran by heart. Ferdowsi, another Persian poet (full name Abul Qasem Ferdowsi Tusi), extolled seeds and the bright sunlight: "everywhere I sow, much have I suffered…" And he added: "Sunlight is my bread." In his poem "Bread and Wine," the German poet and philosopher Friedrich Hölderlin wrote: "bread is the fruit of the earth, yet it is blessed also by light" (*doch ists vom Lichte gesegnet*). It is this verse that I quote early on in this book.

Mahatma Gandhi, who while in exile preached active nonviolence and tried to protect the "untouchables", whom he called "Harijans" – the Children of God – concluded wisely when speaking about faith: "There are people in the world so hungry, that God cannot appear to them except in the form of bread." Thus Christ revealed himself to the world both as a man and as the Son of God.

He was judged and crucified.

There are so many works that describe bread and our relationship with it. For many years now, the human hand has been increasingly replaced by machines, humans by robots and experience by manufacture. Machines now plough, sow, reap, grind and bake. In spite of the imposition of industrialization on our lives, I am reminded of words I once overheard in an

Armenian monastery, at the foot of Mount Ararat: "The land where we were born and grew up imbues us with the taste of its bread, especially in the case of someone who had to leave or who was banished. Nothing can replace it."

The poetics of bread is scattered like grains through time and space, across countries and peoples, in everyday life and eternity. It reveals itself in poetry, paintings and prayer. It is present when dreaming and when awake, "between dreams and reality", in the shortness of an instant and in the length of time.

We carry it within ourselves, knowing it and forgetting it at the same time.

VI.
IMAGES AND
SEMBLANCES

Representations of bread have their place in history and the arts. They can be found traced on stone, wood and metal, drawn on papyrus, parchment and canvas, they can be found in carvings, bas-reliefs and sculptures, in frescoes and wall paintings, mosaics and icons. The history of art has inventoried them in its catalogues and collections. Literature has preserved bread as something real and something imagined.

Since ancient times, there have been religions that proscribe depicting the image of God. Idolatry was condemned in the Law at Sinai and in the Talmud (*Avodah Zarah*). The Ten Commandments declare: "Thou shalt not make unto thee any graven image, nor any likeness of anything that is in heaven above." Later books written in Hebrew, especially those influenced by Kabbalistic and Hassidic teaching, opened up their pages to images of prophets, and of men and women. The *Haggadah* depicts scenes of everyday life, and there one sees all kinds of bread.

In eighth- and ninth-century Byzantium, disputes flared up between iconoclasts and iconodules. Emperor Leo III the Isaurian, who ruled

Byzantium from 717 until his death in 741, banned images of the Lord, the Virgin Mary and saints in all basilicas. In the ninth century, Empress Theodora succeeded in restoring to Eastern Christianity its iconostases. Her stance was supported by the Council of Nicea.

And so bread reappeared on icons, alongside the chalice and the hands of Jesus.

At the Last Supper, Christ broke bread and shared it with his disciples. The supper took place at the beginning of the "Feast of Unleavened Bread", during Easter Week, perhaps on a Thursday, or even a Wednesday, but certainly before Friday when Jesus was crucified. In the Old Testament, Moses ordered the removal of all traces of leaven in commemoration of the days when the Jews fled from the pharaoh's soldiers and in their haste had no time to wait for the bread dough to rise: "Seven days shall ye eat unleavened bread; even the first day ye shall put away leaven out of your houses." For, says the biblical book of Exodus, "whosoever eateth that which is leavened, even that soul shall be cut off from the congregation of Israel, whether he be a stranger or born in the land." Naïve drawings and faded colours depict refuges bending down to collect the manna that had fallen from heaven. The words *matzah* and *hametz* increasingly replaced the old names for bread, *lehem* and *pat*.

The Last Supper became an inspirational motif in medieval and especially Catholic painting and artists strove to depict and interpret it. Giotto's representation of the table laid before Christ does not particularly highlight bread, but it leaves the impression of it being thin and flat, in other words made without leaven. The small bread Leonardo da Vinci places by Jesus' hands looks slightly raised, and the one at the edge of the table in front of Judas even more so. In *Supper at Emmaus*, which also took place on Easter Sunday, Caravaggio depicts an unquestionably raised bread. For Dürer in his woodcut of *The Last Supper*, Tintoretto in his huge painting of *The Last Supper* in the Scuola di San Rocco in Venice, and Rembrandt in *The Supper at Emmaus*, the bread is clearly leavened. And the same is true in the paintings of Bassano, Titian, Nicolas Régnier, Giovanni Bellini and so many other artists. In

"СОЮЗ СОВЕТСКИХ СОЦИАЛИСТИЧЕСКИХ РЕСПУБЛИК
ЕСТЬ СОЦИАЛИСТИЧЕСКОЕ ГОСУДАРСТВО
РАБОЧИХ И КРЕСТЬЯН".
(из конституции советского союза)

VII.
AFTERWORD

The country in which we are born and raised gives us a taste for its bread. When life takes or displaces us elsewhere, we carry that taste with us, inside of us. To lose that taste is to lose a part of your country, and of yourself.

A foreigner arriving in a city for the first time is bound to come across its native bread. Sometimes it is like the bread back home, but sometimes it is different. There where the languages are closer, the bread seems more familiar.

It is hard to grasp all the connections that link language and bread.

Bread raises many questions and elicits all sorts of advice. "Who among you, if his son asks him for bread, would give him a stone?" Or: "It is not right to take the children's bread and toss it to the dogs." These examples come from the Holy Scriptures. We all carry our own story of bread within us.

This, the seventh and last chapter, explains what prompted me, the author, to write this book.

As a child I survived four hungry years living on barely a crust of bread. A war was raging, a world war, the second in the same century. My father had been interned in a camp just because he came from a country that another country was at war with. He had fled Russia twenty years before Germany went to war with his homeland again. He was imprisoned as an ordinary, mobilized soldier in Yugoslavia, where he had emigrated all those years before and which was now collapsing for the first time. Most of the people taken away with him never returned. He, by some miracle, survived. The next time I saw him I barely recognized him. He had lost 90 lb (40 kg) during his internment.

He often told a story about bread in the camp.

The end of 1942 and beginning of 1943 saw one of the harshest winters of the century. In northern Germany, near Osnabrück, my father found himself with a group consigned to do forced labour. They felled trees and trimmed the sleepers for new railway tracks that were wider and better suited for supplying the German troops and conquering territory. One evening, a group of freezing, starving inmates in ragged clothes and wooden clogs was on its way back to the barracks. "We didn't look human anymore. It was as if we had turned into mere shadows of ourselves," my father remembered. They were intercepted on the narrow road by a stranger who invited them to his house. "Accompanied by our guard, we entered the house mistrustfully. It was Christmas Eve. The house was warm."

The man was a Protestant pastor. Following Abraham's example, he gave his unknown guests what he had to offer. First, a chance to warm up, wash and shave. On the table was a slice of bread and glass of wine for each, followed by a simple meal, in keeping with Christian tradition on Christmas Eve. In gratitude, my father sat down at the piano and, his fingers stiff from work and frozen from the cold, played a fragment of an old Russian liturgy.

When the stay was over, the pastor and the inmates embraced each other. The guard did not report any of them. After that day, he never again equated his captors with the nation they came from. "You have to separate the wheat from the chaff," he would say. "Think of everything

that happened in Russia and in Ukraine, in my own native Odessa!"
There were other scenes like that during the war. Too few, but they
happened.

After the war and the camp, my father came home to the small town
where we had taken refuge with some impoverished relatives. It was a
time when captured German soldiers were paraded in the street. They
were treated vengefully, without mercy, and made to do the worst jobs.
You could see from their faces that they were hungry and exhausted.
I remember how their ribs protruded through their ragged clothes. We
had very little ourselves in those days, since the war had taken almost
everything from us, yet there was renewed hope that things would change
for the better.

One day, my father cut in half the loaf of bread that we received twice
a week as our ration for the whole family. "Take this to the German
prisoners. Make sure nobody sees you, or we'll be accused of collaborating." I slipped in between the walking dead, carrying the bread under
my shirt, its crust scratching my chest. I gave it to a tall, thin, blond
German soldier whose eyes welled up with tears. He shared it with two
other prisoners.

I never forgot my father's story about the Protestant priest. Maybe
my desire to write a book about bread one day dates back to then, when
I was a boy. The idea would come and go over the years, but it never
completely disappeared. As I grew older, I don't know how many times
I would start writing and then abandon the whole project, only to pick
it up again. When I emigrated from my country, which had gone to war
with itself, I had other things I had to do. I wrote books of a different kind,
but I never forgot *Our Daily Bread*.

In the early seventies of the last century, I had my first opportunity
to see the Red Sea and to visit Odessa, where my father was born and
from which he had emigrated in 1920 as a twenty-year old. Through the
Red Cross, we obtained the address of one of his cousins, who was old
and sick by the time I met her. Auntie Natalia, known as Tusya, was the
daughter of Mikhail Grigorashenko, hero of the October Revolution
and a doctor who became famous for saving several provinces and cities

from the epidemics that raged after the fighting was over. All the same, she spent five years in a gulag for having spoken her mind about the Holodomor, the terrible famine that claimed so many lives in Ukraine at the beginning of the thirties. Europe's most fertile granary had no grain and approximately 3 million people starved to death. She told me one of the saddest stories about bread I had ever heard:

Apparently, my father's brother Vladimir had disappeared in one of Stalin's camps, accused of communicating with relatives who had emigrated abroad, of spreading "enemy propaganda", and of "collaborating with Trotskyites", with whom he could not have communicated even had he wanted to. Grief-stricken, Grandfather Nikolai nevertheless survived his own gulag, though not for long. My grandmother was devastated and roamed the streets, searching for her sons and her husband. She died on a park bench, having lost her mind. In 1941, during the German siege of Odessa, Grandfather Nikolai used his last ounce of strength to carry modest "rations" of bread to the elderly and infirm, along with messages, though I do not know what they said. Auntie Natalia suggested that I see a man who had been in the camp with my uncle Vladimir, telling me only that he lived in a suburb of Odessa and that his name was Pyotr.

She did not give me his last name. I don't know why. She gave me just his address – his house and flat number.

The man I met was unusual. His face bore traces of suffering, and he would gaze off into the distance, to the side somewhere. He did not speak like everyone else. He told me that Uncle Vladimir died asking for bread, interned somewhere near Saratov. The famous scientist, botanist and grain expert Nikolai Vavilov had been with them for a year or two in the same camp. Vavilov's theory about the origin of the first varieties of wheat in the plateaus of East Africa, in Eritrea, was closer to the work of abbot Gregor Mendel than to the ideas of Ivan Michurin, so extolled by official propaganda. Vavilov refused to carry out orders that went against his convictions. He did not hide the fact that nobody knew if "wheat would ever grow in the steppes of Turkmenistan or tundra of Siberia". Attacked by Trofim Lysenko, Stalin's official "agricultural ideologue" and commissar, Nikolai Vavilov was arrested and sent to the gulag. There he became friends with my Uncle Vladimir and they spent their days and nights together, sharing the odd slice of bread that came their way.

Pyotr spoke very, very softly, as if afraid of being overheard. "You have no idea what it means to want bread when you're in a place like that. Your Uncle Vladimir died with the words 'bread, bread' on his lips!"

I wanted to help the pale-eyed old man in his frayed but clean linen *rubashka* shirt, but he refused the small roll of banknotes that I tried to slip into his pocket. Apologizing, he returned it to me and said that instead of giving him money, I should write him a "letter about bread", the bread he himself had so longed for and that even now was in short supply for his family and friends.

That was at the beginning of the 1970s, when a certain "thaw" could be felt in the air.

I continued my trip through what was then the Soviet Union. I wrote to Pyotr every day, shortening or fleshing out my letter. I wanted to find the right words for this man whose education had been interrupted by prison and the gulag, and for whom prayer had taken the place of books. We later learnt from Natalia that he had received only two or three versions of my letter, after censorship. She eventually managed to correspond with my father in that thaw of the 1970s. Pyotr died soon afterwards. "He took communion with rye bread," she told us.

One of the versions of my letter said the following (translated from the Russian):

I have not travelled the world; my knowledge of bread is modest, said the pilgrim. Bread is to me the world.

Don't cut it, break it in the palm of your hand, were the words of the monk from Rostov-on-Don. Then your prayer will be heard.

There won't be enough bread and salt left to welcome our loved ones. The old woman lived in hope. Her sons had gone their separate ways. She waited for them, alone and pious, in front of the door of the log house.

The most exhaustive book written about bread to date is *Sechstausend Jahre Brot* ("Six Thousand Years of Bread") by Henrich Eduard Jacob, a German Jew. At the end of the book, he writes about his detention in the Buchenwald concentration camp, where he was given bread made out of a "mixture of potato and sawdust". Who knows if Jacob would have written such an important book had he not been in a concentration camp and eaten that kind of bread. Yes, mixed with sawdust, as in ancient times and in the Middle Ages, or with sand, earth, desert dust...

In the course of the seventeen years that I spent "between exile and asylum", in France and in Italy, I also consulted the books and studies of the following: the late Arnaldo Luraschi, the almost forgotten author of *Il pane e la sua Storia* ("Bread and its History"); Massimo Montanari, a colleague and professor at the University of Bologna and the author of "Food: A Culinary History from Antiquity to the Present"; Steven L. Kaplan, the American specialist whose knowledge of French bread is equal to that of the great Poilâne; Gabriel Mandel of Milan, persecuted and interned during World War II for being Jewish, who converted to Islam, became a follower of Sufism and was accorded the title of Khan in the Turkish town of Konya – I found his comments about bread in Sufi poetry invaluable. The "lessons" of Michel Foucault whom I had occasion to meet at the Collège de France, where I occasionally lectured, directed me to the experience of the Hellenic cynics and especially the way they "begged for a piece of bread" in their quest for the truth. Foucault died leaving behind an unfinished manuscript about the uncompromising speech of the cynics, entitled *Parrēsia*.

And I cannot forget my friend from the former Yugoslavia, doctor of science Rajko Djurić, a Rom who lost part of his family in the Nazi camps in World War II, and part in the wars that ravaged the Balkans in the 1990s. It is he who translated the various Roma sayings for me. I also referred to the work of Ihsan Sidhki el-Ahmed, who wrote a historical study of bread in Islamic civilization. The writer Gamal El-Ghitani, considered by some as the "heir to Naguib Mahfouz", sent me the manuscript from Cairo and I found someone in Bosnia to translate it for me, which gave me access to numerous sources in the Arabic language. I also received valued help from two friends and colleagues: the French historian Georges Duby, one of the most original thinkers and writers on land cultivation, and Piero Camporesi, author of *Il Pane Selvaggio* ("Wild Bread"), in the wake of which I wrote the first of this book's seven chapters. Both left us too soon. The Slovene poet Edvard Kocbek, a Christian and personalist, dissident and antifascist, encouraged me at the very start not to abandon writing the book you now hold in your hands.

Since time immemorial, poets, philosophers and scholars have been writing the great saga of bread, each inspiring the other and all making their own contributions. At the dawn of the third millennium, a vast number of people are still dying of starvation, especially in the so-called "Third World", in Asia and Africa, the places where grains first originated,

Climate change and environmental pollution are prompting today's nomads, so-called refugees or economic migrants, to search, sometimes in desperation, for a life in regions where bread is not so scarce. The uncontrolled consumption of energy threatens to have fatal consequences and our planet is suffering from the impact of various devastating phenomena: on the one hand, polar ice caps are melting, sea levels are rising, waves are flooding archipelagos and continents are sinking into the ocean; on the other, vast areas of the world are without enough water, deserts are encroaching on more and more land, droughts are destroying crops and starvation is plaguing people.

As I write these pages, the world is once again in the grip of a crisis. It has swept the world with untold speed, confronting humanity with unheralded threats. Soon the population on our planet will number 8 billion people; according to the experts, one quarter of them could be left without bread. I met the eminent American agronomist Norman Borlaug after he had developed high-yielding, disease-resistant varieties of wheat. His efforts saved the lives of millions of starving people in the so-called "developing countries". Until the day he died he kept warning that "hunger is still a common thing. Hunger is all too frequent."

What can literature do to ensure that there is enough bread for each and every one of us?

It can only express our concern and alarm.

Well before he celebrated his one hundredth birthday, the French anthropologist Lévi-Strauss wrote in his memoir *Tristes Tropiques*, that "the world began without the human race and it will end without it."

The human race began without bread and it could well end without it.

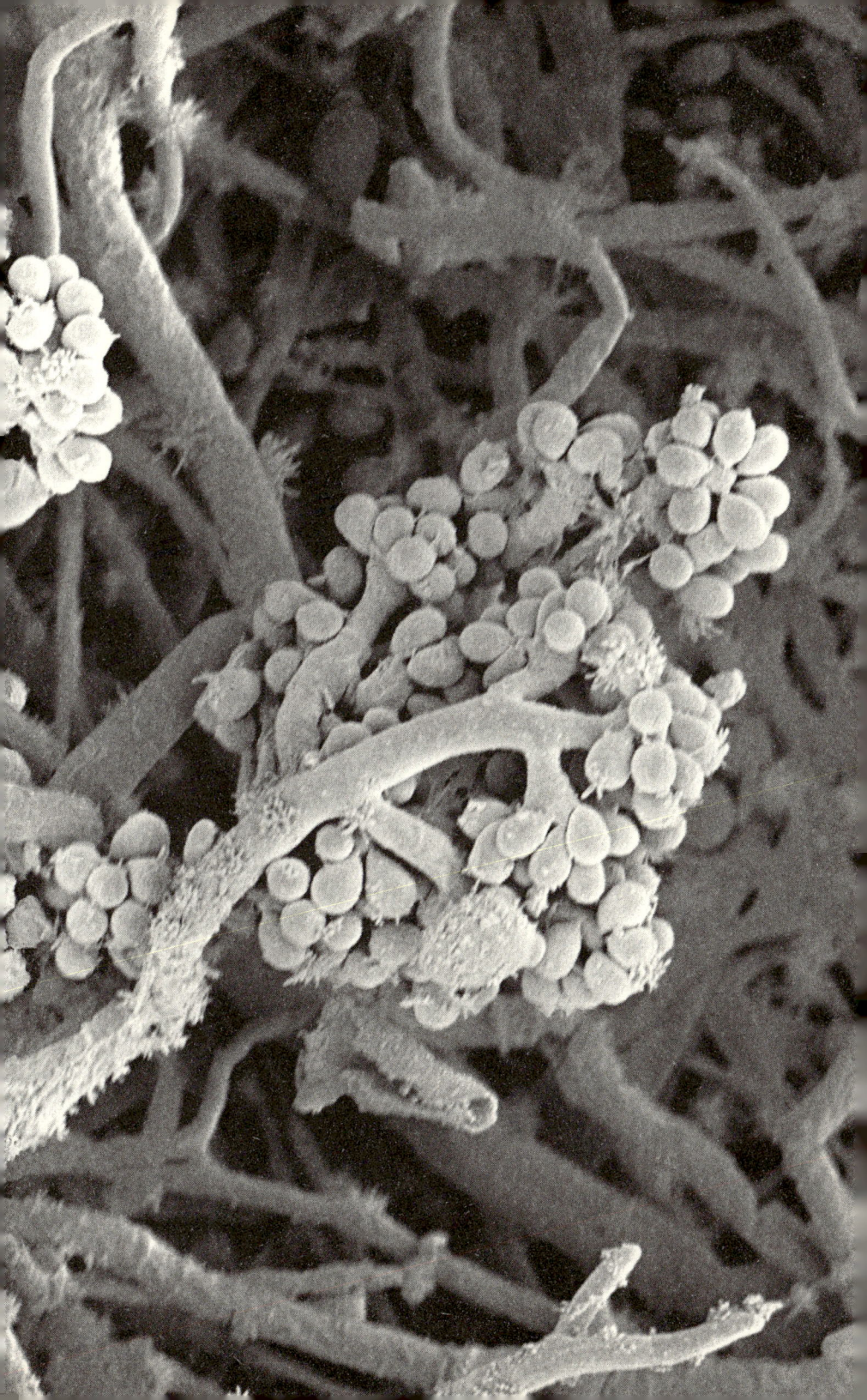

IMAGE CREDITS

his painting *St Hugh in the Carthusian Refectory*, seventeenth-century Spanish artist Francisco de Zurbarán places in front of the Carthusians seated at their refectory table the large loaves of leavened bread that were made in Spain at the time.

Clearly, painters did not follow the prescripts of Moses. The most talented and most inspired among them were more interested in the seating of the apostles around Christ, the gaze of the Son of God, the position of his body at the table, and of his hand and fingers when blessing the bread. This departure from the Old Testament on the walls of churches and in icons was dictated by art itself.

Apart from *The Last Supper* and *Supper at Emmaus*, bread most often figures in depictions of the wedding at Cana, in the biblical scene of the *Multiplication of the Loaves*, and in scenes celebrating the Eucharist.

In all Catholic representations, the host is flat, round and clearly unleavened.

The question of leavened or unleavened bread was posed differently in Byzantium and other Eastern Orthodox countries: Holy Communion invariably used leavened bread. In some of Andrei Rublev's icons, the sacramental bread is so deeply submerged in the gold background that it is barely visible. In the Orthodox liturgy, the *epiclesis* invoking the Holy Spirit seems to give the bread a lighter, more transparent tone. No small number of examples can be found in celebrated schools of icon painting, in monasteries in Greece, Bulgaria, Serbia, Macedonia, Romania and especially on Mount Athos.

The raven, too, has finally found a place next to bread. According to Hebrew tradition, the bird was originally white. Its feathers started turning black after Patriarch Noah sent it forth to see if the floodwaters had receded, but it never came back. Still, in icons the raven is depicted next to the prophet-saint Elijah, St. Anthony the Abbot, St. Paul the Hermit. Every day it carried a morsel of bread in its beak for the anchorites who lived in caves, dedicating their body and soul to fasting and prayer. Diego Velázquez and Albrecht Dürer, among others, depicted the black bird as a benefactor.

Bread is also used for the restoration of palimpsests. The centre of the bread, moistened until soft, is used to clean old canvases, wooden boards and parchment by carefully rubbing it on them to remove the dust and dirt, thus revealing, one by one, the layers that covered the original lines, drawing or colours. And, in the end, we finally see the Virgin Mary or Christ breaking bread, who had been hidden under another superimposed painting.

〽〽〽

The surahs of the Quran do not allow the depiction of any sacred or human figures (*ibada al-asnam*) in art. However, in calligraphy artists introduced ornaments and arabesques reminiscent of the silhouettes of loaves of bread and cakes from their respective regions: round, triangular, rectangular, light and dark. We see them in the Al-Azhar mosque and Abdeen palace in Cairo, in the collections of the Topkapi Palace in Istanbul, in the tombs of the Mamluks and caliphs. We can recognize them in the green and gold swirls that resemble young and mature wheat. There is often a similarity between the rough surface of the wall and the rough crust of the bread.

Neither the authorities nor religion could stop Arab cartographers from drawing, and at times embellishing, the outlines of countries and their coasts. A good example was the celebrated twelfth-century geographer Al-Idrisi of Sicily, known as "the Sicilian" (*Al Siculi*). His work was continued by al-Sharfi in the Mediterranean port of Sfax, in Tunisia. The round and rectangular islands scattered in the sea resemble the little breads that sailors and desert people so loved. Even though religious leaders banned portrait painting, Sultan Mehmed II, known as Mehmed the Conqueror (*fatih*), invited the Venetian artist Gentile Bellini to Istanbul to paint his portrait for posterity. Bellini brought a sigh of the East back to Venice, which was to have an influence on the art of Carpaccio.

〽〽〽

In the wake of the Enlightenment and the French Revolution, secularization saw bread move increasingly from the religious to the secular sphere. Artists emphasized its social importance – the desire and need to give bread to the poor and the starving. More and more often paintings are of the workman with his plough, the sower tossing a handful of seeds, the reaper swinging his scythe. Alongside them are stacks of hay, sheaves of grain, piles of straw and various implements with those who lived side by side – the peasant, the baker, the beggar.

Bread and water, for today and tomorrow. Heavy water does not flow to the sea, said the hermit from Suzdal; we measure our steps, yet we are without measure.

A succession of barren years; the ears of rye lay flat on the ground. We had armies to feed. Bread and love, Vassilisa, for the autumn awaiting us and the winter we will not see.

The loaves made by the young brides of the South were ruined. Collect the crumbs in your kerchiefs, for the fast and communion. The healthy grain will remain in the ground, under the snow.

The vagabond crossed the steppe on the other side of the Yenisei River, off in the distance. Day after day, there is less and less seed. Who will bring this people together? Bread and wine!

A voice called out, loud and clear so that we could all hear him: bread and leaven, brothers! We've been slogging through the mud for a long time. There are still some clear springs to be found.

We sing softly, we can barely hear our own voices: the crust of earth and the crust of bread. Flat and vast is Russia.

That is what I wrote at the end of my letter to Pyotr.

∾∾∾

More books helped me to write these pages than I can list, but some should not be forgotten. I have already mentioned Nikolai Vavilov, all of whose work I have read. He was a candidate for the Nobel Prize but never received it. He died in a Soviet workcamp in Siberia in 1943.

Today, there is an institute bearing his name in St. Petersburg.

Pyotr Kropotkin's book *The Conquest of Bread* was also of great help. In the battle for bread, "need" must take precedence over "duty".

"The question of bread must take precedence over all others," wrote the noble anarchist Kropotkin, dubbed the "black prince".

After my sad stay in Odessa, I began to examine the question of bread from all sorts of aspects – anthropological, sociological, historical, religious, political and even poetical. I read the work of Osip Mandelstam and the tragic memoir of his wife Nadezhda, *Hope Against Hope*. In the first years after the October Revolution, many Russian writers spoke about "conquering bread for all", without pandering to the increasing pressures of the powers-that-be. Mandelstam is the author of the almost forgotten essay *Pshenitsa chelovyecheskaya* ("The Wheat of Humanity"). He wanted to reconcile the "two Eucharists", the religious and the agnostic. He celebrated leavened bread, "like Hagia Sophia ... whose cupolas rise filled with round ardour". He saw bread shine in the ostensorium – the vessel used in Roman Catholic, Old Catholic, High Church Lutheran and Anglican churches for the more convenient exhibition of the consecrated Eucharistic host, which is called *daronositsa* in Russian and *artophorion* in Greek. He admired the beauty of the little round buns called *kolobok* – and Kolobov was Mandelstam's first pseudonym when he was young. Observing the bread dough ferment (*hlebnaya opara*), he wondered how just a piece of that dough – *pripek* – could rise like a mountain. In the forced-labour camps of Siberia, the inmates gave the name *turia* to stale, hard bread which, when dipped in warm, salty water, became "edible". Alluding to this image, Mandelstam warned of the problem that arises when bread is taken out of the oven too soon. On the eve of his arrest, in the mid-1930s, he was still dreaming of the "dear yeast of the world", which could help the world itself to change. His death was described by Varlam Shalamov, a writer who spent almost two decades in the gulag. One day, an inmate stole Mandelstam's daily ration of bread, whereupon the poet cried out: "Bread! They took my bread!"

He died hungry for a piece of bread, and I cannot but be reminded of my uncle Vladimir's similar demise.

In *The Fourth Vologda*, Shalamov wrote the story of the lure of another person's bread: "It was someone else's bread, the bread of my comrade ... It was a three hundred gram ration, cold as a piece of wood.

I raised it to my nose and my nostrils caught the mysterious, barely perceptive scent of bread ... I turned the case upside-down and emptied a few crumbs into the palm of my hand. I licked them up with my tongue; my mouth immediately filled with saliva and the crumbs melted away ... I nipped off three small pieces, little ones, the size of my little fingernail, put the bread in the case and lay down. Then I nipped off little crumbs and sucked them. And I fell asleep, proud that I hadn't stolen the bread of my comrade."

I met Alexander Solzhenitsyn after he had emigrated from the Soviet Union in 1974. He told me that for years after leaving the gulag, every night he would place a piece of bread under his pillow.

The Armenian poet Daniel Varoujan was killed in 1905 during the genocide, one of the first of the twentieth century. At the age of thirty-one, he was pulled off a convoy being taken to a death camp by the Turkish army and was stabbed to death near Mount Ararat, which is celebrated in myth and the biblical tradition . Found in the pocket of his coat was a manuscript entitled *The Song of the Bread*, which was salvaged. Written on one of its blood-stained, crumpled pages was the following:

Swaying in the wind –
under the husks, where rise the kernels,
the moon has poured its pitcher of milk.
Thresher to village, and on to the mill,
surge sweeping seas...
And when brides bake the blessed bread
Let the sound of song rise and spread.

In his book *Se questo è un uomo* ("If This Is a Man"), the Italian writer Primo Levi bore witness to the suffering in Nazi concentration camps. There we encounter those in the barracks who steal bread from each other and those who, dying of starvation, cannot perform the chores assigned to them. They are "slapped from the morning to the evening. The Germans call them 'zwei linke Hände' (two left hands)" before finally killing them.

First published in 2020 by
Istros Books
London, United Kingdom www.istrosbooks.com

Copyright © The estate of Predrag Matvejević 2020

First published as *Kruh naš* by V.B.Z. Zagreb (2009)

The right of Predrag Matvejević, to be identified as the author of this work has been asserted in accordance with the Copyright, Designs and Patents Act, 1988

Translation © Christina Pribichevich-Zorić 2020

Cover design and typesetting: Davor Pukljak, www.frontispis.hr
Image on the cover: Detail from an illustration by
Ephraim Moshe Lilien from *Die Bücher der Bibel*.

Printed by Pulsioprint, France/Bulgaria

ISBN: 978-1-912545-09-4

This publication is made possible by the Croatian Ministry of Culture.

Republic
of Croatia
Ministry
of Culture
Republika
Hrvatska
Ministarstvo
kulture

FREEDOM
TO **WRITE**
FREEDOM
TO **READ**

Supported using public funding by

**ARTS COUNCIL
ENGLAND**

This book has been selected to receive financial assistance from English PEN's "PEN Translates" programme, supported by Arts Council England. English PEN exists to promote literature and our understanding of it, to uphold writers' freedoms around the world, to campaign against the persecution and imprisonment of writers for stating their views, and to promote the friendly co-operation of writers and the free exchange of ideas.

www.englishpen.org